To Laura—

Thank you for

friendship.

Enjoy!

Víctor

Advance Praise for
The Kitchen Table Financial Plan

"In *The Kitchen Table Financial Plan*, Victor Levy creatively demonstrates the value of working with a financial advisor and how financial advice can be the most impactful when the advisor-client relationship is personalized, collaborative, and built on trust."

—DAN ARNOLD, PRESIDENT, LPL FINANCIAL

"Victor S. Levy takes us on more than 'a day in the life' journey from dreams to reality through financial planning. *The Kitchen Table Financial Plan* is not only easy to relate to and understand but takes the mystery out of securing one's future. It's refreshing that these interactions occur at the kitchen table versus in cyberspace. As a physician with little background in business, I found this book a valuable read."

—DR. LARRY I. BARMAT, ABINGTON REPRODUCTIVE MEDICINE

"*The Kitchen Table Financial Plan* answers the question 'How can I put my head on the pillow and know my finances are in order?' If the thought of contacting a financial planner has always seemed an expensive and scary endeavor, then this book is the key to unlocking that mystery. I wish I had read this book early in my working career, as I might have started my financial plan earlier. I will recommend it to all my employees and friends who are still on the fence about having a solid financial future."

—MATTHEW BEES, CEO/PRESIDENT, ADVANCED ABRASIVES CORPORATION

"In *The Kitchen Table Financial Plan*, Victor Levy provides valuable, easy-to-understand guidelines for establishing financial goals, using real-life examples and situations to demonstrate the importance and advantages of working with a financial planner."

—AMY BLACKSTONE

"*The Kitchen Table Financial Plan* is an intimate, personalized view of the world of family financial planning. It presents a realistic picture of how the fears and uncertainties of real people's lives can be transformed into hope and confidence with the help of a financial planner. The real story here, however, is not the finances nor the planning, but the passion, compassion, and love of people and family that the financial planner brings to his profession. This is a must-read for all!"

—DR. ARTHUR CHILDS, DIRECTOR, DR. ARTHUR CHILDS MEDICAL HOME, BOARD CERTIFIED INTERNAL MEDICINE AND CRITICAL CARE

"Using a fictitious couple and their family, Levy reveals in plain language the value and trademarks of a good financial planner. The book addresses the trepidation and procrastination many people experience when faced with managing their money. In the daunting world of finance and tax law, the setting of the kitchen table brings the clients and the planner to a level playing field. The planner and his financial firm 'family' sort out and construct a clear, workable way for the client to achieve their goals. As the extended family encounters life's problems, the planner is a source of support and guidance. This book is an excellent resource for financial planners as well as those in need of such services."

—DR. NEIL COHEN AND DANA COHEN

"Making financial information not only palatable but interesting is not an easy task. Add to that a fictional story about a family learning at the same time, and you have the inspirational and informative *The Kitchen Table Financial Plan*. Victor Levy has created a primer for all stages of financial planning and life . . . a great way to figure out where you are going and if you are doing it the best way!"

—MARSHA Z. DOLLINGER, EDUCATOR

"*The Kitchen Table Financial Plan* is an engaging read. It is personable and filled with relatable life situations. It is a wake-up call to anyone who doesn't use a financial planner."

—J. LEVINE

"I am a physician reading another professional's approach to a different, but somehow similar topic. 'Financial' problems are different than those that I am faced with on a daily basis. However, I see many similarities in the problems that occur and the thought processes of the 'therapists' in this book that are shared by all who are dedicated to making life easier and healthier. How do we gather facts, deal with emotions, look at the consequences of the 'illness,' recommend a plan to remedy the problems, be prepared for ancillary 'fallouts,' keep on a steady course, and help develop a smart thought-out plan for the future? Victor Levy, in *The Kitchen Table Financial Plan* does this well, with insight, understanding, keen professional knowledge, and, most of all, compassion for those seeking help along the way."

—ALVIN D. DUBIN, DO, EXECUTIVE-
VICE PRESIDENT/CEO, AMERICAN
OSTEOPATHIC COLLEGES OF
OPHTHALMOLOGY, OTOLARYNGOLOGY-
HEAD & NECK SURGERY

"*The Kitchen Table Financial Plan* sounds like the biography of our financial experience. It should be required reading for young professionals and their spouses during the first five working years. The financial missteps made by the Bell family in the book are too often the rule rather than the exception. They can and should be avoided with early financial planning. We wish we had started with a professional plan twenty years earlier than we did!"

—JOSEPH E. GIAN-GRASSO, DMD, DIPLOMATE,
THE AMERICAN BOARD OF PERIODONTOLOGY,
FELLOW, THE ACADEMY OF OSSEOINTEGRATION,
AND JANICE GIAN-GRASSO

"I found it riveting to read about financial planning from the planner's point of view. This book gives insights into the thought processes of both the client and the CFP® practitioner, and rings familiar and valid. A highly recommended and easy read!"

—FAYE MERTZ

"All our lives we have heard, 'a penny saved is a penny earned.' *The Kitchen Table Financial Plan* presents a realistic, modern story of what happens when we spend beyond our limits and never consider the rainy day. Victor Levy has created a simple story that we all can relate to when it comes to the realities of unexpected circumstances that come with life—from aging to children growing up. Victor teaches you that saving does not mean you have to be wealthy; it just means you need to have the proper guidance and help in setting up and sticking to a plan for your financial expectations. Most people will be pleasantly surprised at the simplicity a financial plan can bring to your life—whether it's guiding an aging generation or mentoring a young one just starting out."

—ILYA GIRLYA, PRESIDENT, DIGGERLAND USA

"Do you have a financial planner? If not, do you know why? Do you know how to find a financial planner? Do you know what he or she can do for you and how he goes about it? If any of these questions have gone through your mind, then this is the book for you! *The Kitchen Table Financial Plan* explains each question comfortably, concisely, and in depth. This is a multilayer representation of the process of creating a financial plan from start to finish. As the process evolves, your anxiety lessens and your comfort increases. This is a good, comprehensive read that starts at your kitchen table."

—JOSEPH B. ICENHOWER, JR., DMD

"Finally! A comprehensive, easy to understand, personal financial advice manual. Victor Levy has written a user-friendly and practical guide to help navigate complicated financial waters. I'm a busy physician with little time to pay attention to these issues. Mr. Levy has designed his book to be a user-friendly instruction manual, which I found extremely helpful and easy on the eyes!"

—STEVE SOMKUTI, MD, PHD, ABINGTON REPRODUCTIVE MEDICINE

"Uplifting and heart-warming vignettes of a CERTIFIED FINAN-CIAL PLANNER™ practitioner in dealing with real-life situations. The book sets forth the role of a CFP® practitioner as a guiding light to clients as they travel through their battles with financial security and wealth management. A very valuable read for professionals such as accountants and lawyers who only deal on the periphery of their own clients' personal concerns about the financial aspects of life. The book shows how the CFP® practitioner ties everything together, and shows how a CFP® practitioner can lead us in the right direction in meeting our financial goals and dreams."

—MICHAEL JACOBS, CPA, JACOBS
AND ASSOCIATES, LLC

"*The Kitchen Table Financial Plan* is a reflection of how sound financial planning can enhance your life's experiences and prepare you for when life hits you with a curve ball. A complete and thoughtful look at people's lives, both personally and financially, the book shows how providing a financial plan that is reasonable and obtainable will make life experiences better. The book outlines financial life events that may not otherwise be in the forefront of the average person's mind. It's a great read for all ages and we absolutely recommend sharing it with the young people in your life to get them started down the right—and long and happy—road of financial success."

—SAM AND KRISTINA KLICKOVICH

"After a catastrophic car accident, as a single mother of a twelve- and a fourteen-year-old, I found myself, at age forty-two, faced with the task of reinventing my life as I knew it. Had I not sat across the table from my financial planner at age thirty-seven, and planned for the unexpected, I would have lost everything. Victor Levy's style of writing very cleverly presents the importance of creating and implementing a financial plan in a very easy to read and engaging way. I believe the book should be mandatory reading for anyone over the age eighteen, regardless of their current financial status. Victor's beautifully crafted book can help us all better plan our financial futures."

—ABIGAIL SANDLER

"*The Kitchen Table Financial Plan* tells the story of our financial planning experience. We were those people who had never before had a financial planner. This book is an accurate depiction of a good planner's approach to financial planning and, through interactions between the fictional characters in his story, methods and beliefs are well described. It reinforces the meanings of terms used and the purpose of topics covered in planning meetings. It also helps the reader appreciate the many situations a financial planner must consider."

—RALEIGH AND BARRY SELIGER, RETIRED PUBLIC SCHOOL SPEECH AND LANGUAGE SPECIALIST AND RETIRED PUBLIC HIGH SCHOOL TEACHER

"Finally, someone takes the dizzying world of personal finance from the pages of the Sunday business section and distills it into straightforward concepts applicable to everyone from the mailroom to the boardroom. Thank you, Victor!"

—KENNETH SILVER, PRESIDENT, JIM'S STEAKS, SOUTH STREET

"Unfortunately, few of us really understand the need or methodology it takes to create a comprehensive financial plan for the future. *The Kitchen Table Financial Plan* offers the modern family a sensible guide to prepare for future expenses, protect against potential contingencies, and lay the groundwork for financial security that we all desire in our later years. Regardless of whether you are someone who is just beginning a career or are at a point in life when you can finally begin to think about a secure future as your children become independent, this book offers abundant, sensible, and easily understood lessons."

—STEVEN COOK, MD, MEDICAL DIRECTOR/ DIVISION OF OTOLARYNGOLOGY, DEPARTMENT OF SURGERY, NEMOURS/ALFRED I. DUPONT HOSPITAL FOR CHILDREN

THE

Kitchen Table

Financial Plan

A PRACTICAL APPROACH
FOR ANY STAGE IN YOUR LIFE

VICTOR S. LEVY

RIVER GROVE
BOOKS

Published by River Grove Books
Austin, TX
www.rivergrovebooks.com

Distributed by River Grove Books

Design and composition by Greenleaf Book Group and Kim Lance
Cover design by Greenleaf Book Group and Kim Lance
Cover credits: Table Still Life: Thinkstock/iStock collection/karandaey; Gingham Pattern: Shutterstock/Paper Teo

Publisher's Cataloging-in-Publication Data is available.

Hardcover ISBN: 978-1-63299-101-0

Paperback ISBN: 978-1-63299-088-4

eBook ISBN: 978-1-63299-089-1

Printed in the United States of America on acid-free paper

16 17 18 19 20 21   10 9 8 7 6 5 4 3 2 1

First Edition

To my wife and best friend, Suzanne Melissa

Contents

Preface

Where am I going?

I often sit quietly in the early evening and ask myself this question as I reflect upon the events of the day.

Typically, I travel from one house to another with a single goal in mind: I want to help others answer the same question about where they are going.

The work of financial planning when performed at the kitchen table is highly personalized and collaborative. It is about understanding people, or in the professional sense, clients. Where do they want to go in the future and how can I, as a financial planner, help them get there?

Sometimes talk about the future centers around the question of when to stop working. I often hear things like, "I want to retire in fifteen years." At other times, the future is about pursuing a lifelong dream like taking a trip around the world. But then sometimes the future is fraught with fear; people say, "I am concerned about my family's financial security if I should die unexpectedly or become disabled."

Through the use of skills learned in the course of study to become a CERTIFIED FINANCIAL PLANNER™ practitioner and my own life experiences, I help others pursue their dreams. In a sense, I am a dream collaborator; I put together strategies and recommendations to help make other people's dreams come true.

It is very satisfying to meet someone, get to know them, understand their goals, and then execute an appropriate plan. Most of the time, the work takes place in the very center of the client's home, in the heart of it, seated at the kitchen table. It is here, in this comfortable realm, where all things are possible. Big decisions can be discussed, people can ponder challenges and opportunities, perhaps share a cup of coffee and a piece of cake, and freely voice their concerns. The planner must be present with his client, for without presence, dreams will remain simply dreams and the soul of a plan will never be born.

I stand true to this—that a financial plan is more than graphs about the future, or number crunching; it is about understanding the future and working together with others to help them strive toward their dreams.

The following is a story about members of a fictional family, who, with the help of a financial planning professional, put their finances in order so their hopes and dreams can become realities. It is the story of how a financial planner remains present throughout the development, implementation, and eventual monitoring of a financial plan.

For me, the story answers that nagging question: Where am I going?

The answer is simple: I am heading to the next kitchen table.

PART ONE

The Financial Plan

CHAPTER 1

The Sale of *Serving Coffee*

Greg took a step backward in his small art studio, almost tripping over a coffee tin full of brushes as he placed the final, finishing swash of oil paint on his most recent work. The painting, which he'd titled *Serving Coffee*, was from the perspective of the server. He'd painted a pair of arms extending from each of the lower corners of the canvas to a tray filled with seven coffee cups. In the distance, seven well-dressed guests were seated around a table shaded by a tree as they waited to be served.

Greg was a sophomore at the University of the Arts in Philadelphia, and for him, the painting exuded a sense of giving and love, of kindness and caring, all displayed in a rich green and yellow composition. His father, Dr. Thomas Bell, took Greg's painting to his dental office in downtown Vineland, New Jersey, where he displayed it on a wall in the waiting room. Dr. Bell thought his patients might enjoy looking at it, and thought perhaps someone would even want to buy it. He suggested that Greg come up with a price tag for the work of art.

Over the course of several weeks, the painting garnered much praise from Tom's patients. Some said that the painting was "museum quality" and that Greg had "a wonderful knack for colors." But, despite the compliments, there were no buyers.

Until one day, when an older gentleman came to the office for a tooth extraction. He arrived a few minutes early and was seated directly across from *Serving Coffee* in the waiting room. He'd selected a magazine to read, but he couldn't stop admiring the colors and genial composition of the painting. He found that it invited him in, with those serving arms reaching outward, almost hugging the viewer.

He went back to the magazine but kept looking up, distracted by the painting. Finally, he stood up, read the price tag, and took a more careful look at the artwork. After a minute, he nodded and approached the receptionist to inquire about the painting and the painter.

She told him about Greg, Dr. Bell's youngest son; she said he was a college art student, and that his dream was to become a full-time artist. The man's decision to purchase, however, came only after she shared a secret hidden in the canvas. In the distance, seated among the guests, Greg had drawn himself. The artist himself appeared in the art.

The gentleman loved the humor and irony of the fact that the artist, as the creator, also saw himself as the subject matter. This theme resonated with him so resoundingly that he wrote a check on the spot made payable to Greg Bell for the stated price of $1,875. He handed it to the receptionist, and after the appointment, Dr. Bell helped carry the painting to his patient's car. As the men warmly shook hands, Dr. Bell felt very proud that his son had sold his first major work of art.

When Greg returned home after his evening classes, he

found an envelope labeled with his name on the kitchen table. He was astonished to find the check inside. For the first time in his life, he'd sold a painting. The payment seemed to justify his work as an artist and signified that becoming an artist indeed could be a career; the payment told him that his passion to paint could become his livelihood.

Throughout dinner, Greg discussed many ideas for projects that had been circling in his head. "I'll start my own studio," he said with excitement, "and give you more artwork, Dad, to hang on the wall in my lucky spot. It'll be great, you'll see. I have so many ideas!"

As he helped clean up the dishes after dinner, Greg asked his parents what they thought he should do with the check.

Linda looked at Tom, who shrugged his shoulders, and then she looked back at her son. "I think you should deposit it in the bank," she said.

"Sounds good," Greg said. "Can you help me make the deposit? I'm jammed with schoolwork this week."

"Sure thing," Linda said, "I'll take it over tomorrow."

Later that night, as Tom and Linda were preparing to go to bed, they discussed the check. "I think he should keep the money in his savings account," Linda said. "I mean, why should he spend it?"

"Let him spend it. C'mon. You only live once!" Tom said.

They got in bed, and Linda turned off the lamp on the nightstand. In the darkness, she asked Tom for his opinion about the check once again. She was hoping for an acknowledgment that they should encourage Greg to save his money, but none came. Finally, Tom yawned and said impatiently, "Whatever you think is fine. I really don't care what he does with it. If you want him to save it then fine, let him save it. I'm going to sleep now."

After a moment of silence, Tom said, "I love you, Honey." And then, he rolled onto his side.

Linda was still awake, thinking in the darkness. Under her breath she murmured, "I love you, too."

CHAPTER 2

Tom and Linda Bell

Dreams are like shooting stars: They flare brightly, then fade away. For people who live life without a moment's pause, dreams constantly circle. These people can find neither the time nor the inclination to write their dreams down, let alone plan out a strategy to achieve them.

As Tom pulled his car into the office parking lot before work on a Tuesday morning, a dream flashed through his mind. The radio was playing "Surfin' U.S.A." by the Beach Boys. He sat for a moment in his parking space and turned up the volume. When the song reached the third verse, the one about waxing down surfboards and being gone for the summer, Tom closed his eyes and started dreaming.

He saw himself on a beach, in a baggy bathing suit, in sunny California with a surfboard planted in the sand next to him. From the expression on his face, he didn't have a care in the world. He had retired from work and had traded in his dental probes for sunglasses and a cool drink. As a sense of happiness spread through his body, he began to tap the dashboard in time to the music.

The song faded and commercials began, and, *poof*! As quickly as it had entered his mind, the dream was gone. He turned off his car and walked up the steps into the office, with the strains of "Surfin' U.S.A." still running through his brain.

He mumbled "Good morning" to the staff. The two dental hygienists who had been with him for more than twenty years were getting their work areas prepared for the day.

Tom put his gym bag underneath his desk. He brought it with him each day in the hope that he would find time after work to stop at the gym for exercise. But on most days, this goal would come and go like another expendable dream.

As he sat down and looked over the day's schedule, he rubbed his lower back and let out a sigh. It appeared to be a busy day: four major procedures, along with eleven checkups. At age fifty-five, the days were beginning to feel long, often before they'd begun.

On the one hand, Tom was pleased that his practice was successful, but on the other hand, his stamina was waning. Dentistry was physical; it took endurance to make it through the days. There was no time to think about the future, let alone retirement. Tom lived very much in the moment.

The Buddha might applaud this way of living. However, Tom was neither a Buddhist, nor consciously choosing to live this way. For him, the future was simply tuned out by a busy calendar that did not allow time for anything other than focusing on the present. The future for him was simply the length of time it took to fill a cavity or to place a gold crown on the mount of a decaying tooth. Tooth pain was like that, too; it existed in the here and now.

A staff member walked briskly past Tom's desk with a plunger. "We need to call the plumber," she said.

"What?" Tom said looking up. "What happened?"

"The toilet won't flush," she replied. "I think it needs to be looked at. The darn thing must be over a hundred years old."

Tom had a sudden memory of the first day he'd started his practice, Bell Dental Arts, nearly thirty years ago in downtown Vineland. Tom and Linda moved there just after Tom finished dental school. Tom had made a single visit to a real estate office to get help finding a location. The real estate agent suggested a spot near a new housing development along a main corridor, to which Tom had said, "Fine."

So he landed on East Landis Avenue, which was the expanding end of "Main Street" in Vineland. A refurbished Victorian home there that had previously been a chiropractor's office was the place the agent thought would be a perfect place to start his practice. The only modern part of the property was a hardwired alarm system.

As he and the agent stood in the foyer, he nudged her with his elbow and said, pointing to the alarm keypad, "Pretty fancy, huh?" She smiled, and shortly after Tom opened his doors, she became one of his first patients.

This was how things went in Vineland, which was a community of people who cared about their town, supported local businesses, and loved the beautiful farmland that surrounded the center of the city. This was reflected in the city motto: "A Harvest of Opportunities in the Heart of the Northeast."

Indeed there had been plenty of opportunities for Tom when he opened Bell Dental Arts. His practice was efficient; it ran with just the two hygienists, along with one full-time and one part-time dental assistant, and a receptionist who served as a part-time bookkeeper.

Every year, around tax-filing season, his accountant, Mack Fletcher, would say that everything looked good financially. "You paid your estimates on time and should get back a small refund from the IRS." Then Mack would put his arm around Tom with a smile and say, "Do yourself a favor, Tom. Don't spend it—just put it in the bank."

But Tom was a chronic spender. Although he worked hard and always had money in his checking account, he loved to spend it, mainly on the accoutrements of an affluent life.

For example, he and Linda lived in a restored home that was once Linda's childhood home. It was on a pleasant street, on thirty acres, just about a mile outside the center of town. Since buying it from Linda's mother, they spruced up the inside with various furnishings, custom-built entertainment units, and built-in appliances. On the outside, the landscaping was meticulously maintained.

Tom also spent money on expensive cars, with upgraded leather seats and larger horsepower engines. On weekends, he and Linda drove to Philadelphia and shopped for custom-made shirts and designer shoes at clothing boutiques. In fact, Linda's shoe collection was so vast that they had converted their daughter's old bedroom into a walk-in closet with shelving on all the walls to hold her treasured footwear.

Linda and Tom had two children. Greg still lived with them, and their daughter, Jessica, who was ten years older than Greg, lived nearby with her spouse, Nicole, and their three children. Jessica, like her father, was a practicing dentist in Vineland; however, her specialty was pediatric dentistry.

The receptionist's voice interrupted Tom's reverie. "Dr. Bell, don't forget you have an implant procedure this afternoon."

Tom flipped his calendar ahead a few pages and noticed the block of time off he'd planned to take was approaching. He and Linda loved to travel and went on at least three vacations per year. They traveled extensively throughout Italy, sometimes on private tours, staying in the best hotels and dining in five-star restaurants. Their travel agent prepared elaborate itineraries for them, with warmer destinations in the winter months and European travel in the spring and summer. Upon arrival at the Ritz-Carlton in Puerto Rico recently, Tom and Linda were greeted by name.

He put the calendar down and walked over to the closet to inventory his dental supplies. He liked to handle the restocking in the morning before patients arrived. The implant materials were beginning to run low, and they'd need to be reordered. He scratched his head in disgust as he flipped through the dental supplies catalog. Costs for everything were rising.

When it came to his own needs, or Linda's, Tom typically spent without a fleeting care or concern. His financial planning consisted of a look ahead at his next week's patient loads; if he was busy, he felt secure that his personal spending could continue. Tom's motto was "Live life to the fullest." For his many years in practice, this had felt like a comfortable, sensible way to live.

Linda spent most of her week doing errands and volunteering in the community. She would run from the dry cleaner to pick up Tom's shirts and suits, then to the bank, and then to the club, where she'd often meet her friends for lunch. Afternoons were spent shopping for new outfits or new decorations or necessities for the house.

Wherever she went, she was greeted warmly by merchants, most of whom knew her by name. She made it a point to always say hello—especially at the First Bank of Vineland, where she was a regular. She stopped by at least once a week to make a withdrawal and would often visit with the floor manager to talk about local news or their grandchildren.

Tom and Linda's life was a good one, but despite the many places they traveled to, and the things they acquired for their home, they always desired more. They wanted a bigger house, more expensive cars, and travel to more exotic locations. In fact, a few years before, Tom was considering a stay on Sir Richard Branson's private Necker Island in the Caribbean, which he thought would make "a helluva good story."

A big part of the Bells' spending was on credit. They leased cars, charged vacations, and borrowed to pay for Jessica's and Greg's college tuitions. As the bills came in, Tom would take distributions out of the practice account in order to keep the cash account at the bank full enough to pay their personal bills. He knew Linda would worry about having enough cash in the bank; but as long as it was replenished, everything was in check.

Linda and Tom had a system for the bills that arrived each week: Bills from credit card companies, leasing companies, and furniture financing companies went into one pile; house bills such as mortgage and utilities went into a second pile; and insurance bills went into a third pile. Linda was the "organizer" and Tom was the "payer." Once a week, usually over lunch in the office, Tom sat at his desk and made the payments.

On occasion, Linda would open up a credit card bill after a busy spending period and ask Tom about it.

"Tom, are we OK?" she'd say. "I just looked at the Visa bill and it's over $15,000!" Tom would take the bill from his wife, and with a hug of reassurance, say, "No worries, my love . . . all is well."

————

It was time to start the day. Tom looked at his watch and jumped into Operatory One to greet his first patient.

"Good morning, Phil, how are your folks doing?" asked Tom, as his patient settled into the dental chair.

There were different profit centers in Tom's practice. For example, he made a small profit on cleanings performed by the hygienists. His accountant would explain that although this was Tom's smallest area of profit, it was one of the most important services because it brought patients into the office. Once they were in, it gave Tom a chance to do a check-up, which would often lead to higher-cost services like fillings and caps. The real profit was made in the procedures.

Among all the procedures Tom performed, the most profitable was the dental implant. Many of Tom's patients were elderly and beginning to lose their teeth. When teeth were beyond saving, the protocol was to replace the lost tooth, or maybe several teeth, with a prosthetic. Nearby dentists thought of him as a specialist in implants, and he received many referrals to do that procedure.

It was a point of pride, however, that Tom favored prevention as the best route. Implants and dentures were always the last resort. He told his patients that the best course was a good defense around tooth care, which included regular brushing and flossing.

Tom only wished it was as easy to prevent personal phone calls during procedures as it was to prevent cavities with good hygiene. Right in the middle of a tooth-bonding procedure, his receptionist tapped on his shoulder and said, "Dr. Bell, your wife's on line two, and she said it's important."

Tom sighed deeply into his protective facemask. His rubber-gloved fingers were pushing down on the lower jaw of his patient's mouth, as he'd been examining the tooth he'd been bonding. He moved the overhead light to the side, and pulled off his mask.

"Phil, I'm sorry to have to do this to you," he said, "but I'll be back in just a minute."

In his office, he pulled off one of his rubber gloves with a loud snap, and then picked up the phone.

"What's going on?" Tom said.

"I'm sorry to bother you in the middle of the morning," Linda said, "but we have a major problem."

Tom sat down in his office chair and prepared for bad news. For Linda, calling during patient hours meant that someone must have died or been seriously hurt.

"OK, what is it?"

"We have no money in our bank account," Linda said. Her voice quivered.

Tom was silent for a moment.

"So, I'll transfer money in," he finally said.

"Tom, this was so embarrassing. When I found out, I spoke to Rhonda at the bank because I thought they had made some mistake. But she said that this whole month our balance has been below $1,000."

"Really?" Tom said.

"Yes, really," she said, losing her temper. "Do you think I'm making this up?"

Tom knew the line separating anxiety from anger was quite thin; he was careful not to cross it—especially in the middle of a day packed with patients. "Honey, calm down," he said. "I'll move some money into our checking account from our credit line."

"That's not an option," Linda replied.

"What do you mean that's not an option?" Tom said. His voice was raised and he was becoming angry.

"Rhonda said we have no other accounts to move money from."

"What?" Tom said with loud astonishment.

Tom's receptionist hurriedly walked to his office and closed the door.

"She told me that our credit line was at its maximum and our savings accounts were at a zero balance." Linda was in a full panic, and struggled to get the words out.

"That's absurd," Tom said. "As soon as I am done here I'm calling the bank. Something's not right."

"Tom, wait. Before you go . . . What should I do right now? I need cash for today."

"For now, I can transfer money over from the office account. I know I have a little cushion there," Tom reassured her. He stood up. It was time to get back to his patient.

"But Tom, this is the first time we'd ever dropped to zero in all of our accounts. What happened?" Her voice was anxious.

"I guess I forgot to move money into our account. I don't know," Tom huffed.

"But, Tom—"

"What can I say?" he barked. "Look, honey, I'm sorry!" Tom's face was crimson. With these words, both hygienists stopped what they were doing and got up to investigate. Clustering in the hallway, his staff looked at one another in bewilderment.

On the phone, Linda still probed for an answer. "Is everything OK at the office?"

"Everything is fine," Tom said. "I'm busy as hell right now, and I gotta go."

In truth, however, Tom's income had slowed down recently. As federal interest rates rose, credit in general was tightening; hence all of the dental insurance carriers Tom had relied upon for income reimbursement were delayed in paying Tom for his services. Simply making payroll each week had become a challenge.

"Tom," Linda began, "I think what we should—"

But Tom interrupted her. "Listen, honey, I can't talk about it right now." He spoke calmly, and took a deep breath. "Trust me, the waiting room is packed and my schedule today is full. I will call the bank as soon as I come up for air."

Linda was quiet. Tom checked the phone to see if its light was still on.

Just before he hung up, he asked, "Where are we going for dinner tonight?"

Linda paused before answering. "The Jade Tree at seven o'clock."

"That's right. I'll meet you there. It's a plan." As Tom got up to return to his patient, the handle of the gym bag he had tossed under his desk earlier in the morning looped onto his foot. He tried to shake it off but he couldn't. He got frustrated, reached down to pull it off, and with a struggle, finally removed it. He threw the bag in the bottom of his office closet and slammed the door shut. As he walked hurriedly back to his patient, he placed the facemask over his nose and mouth and muttered to himself, "It's a plan . . . it's a plan . . . it's a plan."

CHAPTER 3

At the Restaurant

When Tom arrived at the restaurant, Linda was already seated, and was perusing the menu. Tom kissed her on the cheek and sat down.

"Hello, Tom," she said. Her voice was stiff and formal. From their earlier conversation, Tom knew she was still upset about their finances.

"Listen, I called Rhonda today," he said. "I had her raise our line of credit. It's my fault, I probably should have done this a while ago."

Linda just kept her eyes on her menu as if disinterested in his words. When she finally looked up, she said, "So, is it done?" Her tone of voice was suspicious.

"Well, I started the application over the phone. It takes a few days to complete," Tom said.

"Oh, I see." Linda looked back at her menu.

"In the meantime, I transferred $5,000 from my business account into our personal account."

"Good," Linda said, then closed her menu. "Is that it?"

Tom was taken aback by her cool demeanor. "Yes, I suppose so," he replied.

"Well then, let me tell you what I did today," Linda said in a tone that sounded as if she was about to make an announcement.

"All right," Tom said as he put his napkin on his lap, getting ready for more news—news he figured was probably not good.

"After we spoke this morning," Linda said, "I made a few calls. The first was to our CPA, Mack Fletcher."

It was not like Linda to call Mack. Tom felt like he was being reported. "Oh, really? And, who else did you call?"

"Peggy." Peggy Abramowitz was an old friend. A recent widow, Peggy was about ten years older than Linda, and Linda looked to her from time to time for advice. She liked the way Peggy did things. "Tom, I have been worried all day. In fact, I find myself worrying a lot about our finances lately."

"Really? What did Mack say?" Tom said. He looked down and smoothed his napkin over his legs.

"He said it sounded as though we could use a financial planner."

"Oh, really," Tom said again, this time sarcastically. Tom had always handled the finances. He saw no need to spend money on a service like this when he could handle the finances adequately by himself. After all, he'd taken care of the problem with the bank earlier in the day.

"Mack recommended a firm here in Vineland. Their name is …" Linda pulled a yellow sticky-note from her pocketbook and read it. "Morgan, Hushingbuck & Foster. I actually called them today and spoke to a very pleasant woman named Joanne. She asked me a few questions, and I made an appointment for us to meet with one of the principals, Larry Morgan, next Thursday at our house."

Tom's face turned red, and his napkin fell to the floor. "What? You made an appointment? Without checking my schedule?"

"Relax, Tom. Please try and control yourself," Linda glanced nervously around the restaurant.

"Did you check to see if I am free next Thursday?" Tom said in consternation.

"Of course I called your office first, and yes, you are free. I was told that it was actually a perfect day because you are doing some big procedure in the early afternoon and you'll want to head out as soon as you're done."

"Oh, OK," Tom muttered sheepishly.

In a businesslike tone, Linda continued. "Mr. Morgan is going to come over to our house to talk to us about what he does, and we'll see if he and his firm can help us. Joanne said he is a CFP® professional or CERTIFIED FINANCIAL PLAN-NER™ professional." She put the yellow slip back in her purse and closed it, then set it on the floor.

"Well, then I guess we're good," Tom said dismissively. He reached for his water. "Was there anything else?"

"After I spoke to Mack, I called Peggy."

"Uh huh," Tom said blankly, still sulking over his disrupted schedule.

"She said she's still working through things. You know, it's been hard for her because Leonard handled everything. She told me that before he died, she knew nothing about their finances. It's taken her a long time to get organized."

Tom glanced down and noticed a stain on his necktie. He picked his napkin off the floor, dabbed it into the water glass, and started wiping his tie. Linda kept talking. "Oh, and Tom, guess who she turned to for help to get organized?"

"I don't know, Dr. Phil?" Tom looked up at Linda and tapped his chin.

"Tom, stop it," Linda said, and laughed for the first time all day. It made Tom feel a little better. Linda then told him that Mack had referred Peggy to the same financial planning firm, and it had worked out very well. She added that Peggy thought Mr. Morgan was very knowledgeable about all things related to finances, and his whole firm was attentive and caring.

But Tom worried about paying for things he didn't value. "Did she happen to mention anything about the cost?" he asked. "Is it expensive to have a financial planner?"

By his question, Linda could tell he wasn't sold on hiring a financial planner. She felt offended that he questioned the cost. Tom spent money on all kinds of things, many of which she thought were ridiculous. Like last week, when he'd spent $5,000 to prune the trees at the house because he didn't like the way the branches looked through the kitchen windows.

The reality was that Linda interpreted Tom's question about cost to mean that if hiring a financial planner was too costly, he would not support it. But she was convinced that they needed one. She was fifty-four, and Tom was fifty-five; she was determined that at this time in their lives, they needed to get their finances under control.

For Linda, having money and savings meant having security. Tom had a good job and made a good living. In fact, Mack told her that Tom's net income last year totaled $578,000, which was about an average year for him. However, despite this level of income, she realized that she and Tom had nothing in the bank to show for it. They had practically no savings or significant investments. Realizing the extent of their disorganization that morning in the bank had frightened her.

After she left the bank, she got in her car and cried. As she sat there with her head on the steering wheel, she thought back to when she was a little girl. She could hear her mother's voice telling her to take the money she had made from her lemonade stand and put it in her piggy bank. "Don't spend it," her mother would say as Linda ran up the stairs. "Save it for a rainy day." She remembered the clinking of the coins as they dropped through the little slot on top.

Linda's mother, Helen Drusselovsky, was a very proud person. She and her husband had left Russia and arrived in America in the late 1950s. They started a small business making wire frames for lampshades. The business did well and provided Helen and her two daughters with a comfortable life. Linda's mother told her to always remember to put away a little side money, just because "you never know what's going to happen." In fact, Linda remembered that her mother would place money in little hiding places around the house. This was her *"knipple"* she said. Then, one day, Linda's father came home early from work. He walked into the kitchen and announced that he'd lost the entire business in a poker game. Helen and her sister were told to go to their rooms. Linda hid under her bed, frightened, as her mother and father screamed and shouted in the kitchen. If it hadn't been for her mother's secret stash of money—her knipple—the family would never have survived.

"Linda, hello, are you still with me?" Tom said.

"What?" Linda looked across the table at Tom.

"I asked you what Peggy said about the cost. Was it expensive?"

"Tom," Linda said, "as far as cost is concerned, the answer is no, I did not ask her what the cost was because frankly, I don't care."

Tom could see the determination in his wife's face. "We need financial planning. We have no major savings, and that's that."

Tom tried to explain that they did have some savings, but Linda was on a mission. She snapped open her menu, with a fleeting thought of how much she'd sounded like her mother. Tom could see that her mind had been made up.

"OK, but . . ." Tom began.

"By the way," Linda said, interrupting him, "We have some work to do before our meeting."

"Work? What kind of work?" Tom said apprehensively.

"We've got to get our statements together." Linda bent down and reached into her purse. "Hold on," she said as she pulled out a piece of paper, "I printed out the email sent to me from their office. I have it right here." Linda unfolded the paper and read from it. "We need copies of our investment and bank statements, tax returns for the last two years, copies of life insurance, disability insurance, long-term-care insurance, health insurance, group insurance through work, pension and 401(k) plan information, IRAs, wills and trusts—and the list goes on." She perused the paper one more time and returned it to her pocketbook. "Oh, and one more thing I guess you can do," Linda said casually.

"What's that?"

"They want to see our expenses by month for the last two years." Tom looked down at his glass of water. He was embarrassed at the thought of sharing all of this personal information with people he didn't know. He was an established dentist in the community. Would word get out that he and Linda were living beyond their means? It was clear that this dinner had become a kind of intervention. "That's a lot of information to put together so quickly. How the hell am I supposed to do that? Tell me!" he said.

Linda looked over the menu, unaffected by Tom's histrionics.

Tom snapped open his menu and mulled over his predicament as he looked at the sushi options. It was hard to argue with his wife about her perception of their apparent need. It was true that they were not organized and his cash flow had tightened. He wondered whether this was something professional help could even address, as the insurance companies that reimbursed him for services moved at their own speed.

For the second time that day, an image flashed through his mind of a sunny beach, a lounge chair with a book on it, and a cool drink on a little table next to the chair. He saw himself staring into an imaginary ocean, relaxed, with no worries or concerns about his finances. Perhaps it was Necker Island after all. Tom sat up in his chair. He looked around.

"Tom? Are you OK?" Linda said. "You look like you're daydreaming. And what's with that smile? You look possessed."

He folded his hands and said, "I'm looking forward to our little meeting with Mr. Morgan." Then he reached across the table and took his wife's hand. With that touch, a feeling of love passed through both of their bodies like electricity—a spark that comes when people are about to gain control of something elusive . . . like a dream.

CHAPTER 4

Meeting Preparation

The rain splattered against the window of the conference room. Larry Morgan and his partner, Paul Hushingbuck, were meeting to talk about their new referral, Linda and Thomas Bell.

"How was your drive to work today?" Paul asked.

"My drive was OK, but I had trouble navigating the parking lot," Larry replied.

"Why, what happened now?" Paul said with a grin.

"Well, I was carrying my briefcase in one hand and some files in the other, and I misjudged the front steps of the office. So I tripped and fell down and all of my papers went flying."

Paul laughed, then composed himself, and said, "I'm sorry. Are you OK?"

"I am, but the financial plans and my elbow both got bruised a bit." Larry chuckled as he rubbed his arm.

Just then, their administrative assistant, Joanne, popped her head into the room and asked if anyone wanted coffee. Joanne was an important part of the team, always keeping things moving along.

Larry was fifty years old, with gray, thinning hair, which he kept short-cropped and neatly combed. Every day he wore a suit, usually either gray or blue, with black shoes and a necktie that was not too colorful but not too drab. He attributed his choice of attire to his parents who taught him early in life that if you were going to handle people's money, you needed to present yourself properly and look the part of a professional. When Larry balked at wearing suits in the beginning of his career, his mother tried to ease his mind about it. "Try to think of your clothes as 'the costumes of life,'" she told him.

His father, who worked for an insurance company in a sales position, acknowledged that he always found that he "thought better" when he wore a necktie. Both of his parents also taught him to be organized. Larry learned from a young age that everything has a place—shoes belonged in the closet on the lower shelves, socks in the top drawer, and books in the bookcase. Likewise, putting things in their proper places applied to people's finances as well.

However, the most important lessons his parents taught him came from their values. Larry's father taught him to show appreciation for others, to show sincerity when taking on tasks, and above all else, to be kind and courteous. His mother taught him how to be a good listener. "Always practice the art of listening," she often reminded him. "Listening is an activity, like playing tennis or anything else. It takes energy and effort."

Larry's partner, Paul, was about ten years younger than Larry, but shared similar values. He was reliable, trustworthy, and extremely kind. He knew intuitively what it meant to be part of a service business, how the essence of the job was the quality of the service, the organization of the details, and the importance of listening to people. He also understood that financial planning took hard work, and Larry and Paul were very hard workers.

When Paul first teamed up with Larry ten years earlier, they'd operated out of a small shared office space under the business name of Morgan Financial Planning. Within two years, as they became busier with new clients, they realized they needed help with the most time-consuming part of financial planning, which was portfolio management; so they decided to hire a seasoned, full-time investment analyst named Barbara Foster.

Barbara was ten years older than Larry and twenty years older than Paul. Born in the Philippines, she was raised in Bucks County, Pennsylvania. Larry recruited her from a large investment firm where she'd acquired significant experience in managing assets. Choosing stocks, bonds, and mutual funds was stressful work, but Barbara loved to do it.

They renamed the firm Morgan, Hushingbuck & Foster. It sounded like a law firm, Larry thought. His vision was to present to the community of Vineland a team of associates whose main goal was to help clients pursue their financial goals. With their newly rebranded identity, the firm searched for new office space. They settled on a refurbished office along the west end of Landis Avenue. It had originally been a home, and like the psychologist's office that flanked it to the left and the optometrist's office on the right, the office gave the appearance of being homey. Larry embraced this feeling fully. He felt that managing people's financial lives should feel very much like it was being done at their kitchen table.

Larry stopped rubbing his bruised arm and took a sip of coffee Joanne had brought him. "Paul, let's talk about the Bells," he said.

"That's why we're here," Paul said. He reached for the file tabbed "Linda and Thomas Bell," which Joanne had placed on the conference room table.

Everyone in the office had a special role; Joanne's professional training was that of a Registered Paraplanner^{SM} or RP®. Joanne specialized in providing administrative support to financial planners, analogous to a paralegal in the legal profession. In the new client file, Joanne included a fact-finding packet, a risk tolerance questionnaire, and a brochure about the firm.

Larry was particular about the way he conducted a first meeting. His goal was to get to know his clients, not to simply spend time completing forms. Larry believed that a first meeting should breathe, and the conversation should flow freely. Despite the loose pace, the preparation ahead of the meeting was critical.

The pre-meeting process was usually the same. Paul and Larry would meet a few days before to discuss what they knew about the potential client. They would compile a list of discussion topics, which served as a way to control the pace of the meeting. Paul would typically write these down and prepare them in a formal agenda.

Larry was a believer in the idea that if he could set out his meeting goals in writing ahead of time, his mind would "steer" him through the planning process. He followed principles set forth by Dr. Maxwell Maltz in the book *Psycho-Cybernetics*. Maltz wrote of the "steersman" that existed in the human brain and can be used for goal setting and achievement. "You must plan to plan," was a favorite expression of Larry's in this regard.

"Let's go over what we know," Larry said. He wrote the word "Facts" on a dry-erase board with a blue marker, then turned back to look at Paul. Paul perused some notes he'd taken during a call he and Larry had placed to Mack Fletcher shortly after they received Linda's call.

"The Bells are married and have two children," Paul said, reading from the file. "Tom is a dentist with a successful practice, and Linda, Tom's wife, is not working at this time, but is a nurse by training. One child, a daughter, is a dentist like her father, and the other, a son, is an art student in a local college. Mack said that Tom's cash flow from the practice was favorable, but he thinks they struggle with saving money. He said he knew them to be very thoughtful and generous people."

Larry wrote down all of the key elements on the board. "Do you recall if Mack mentioned whether they had ever worked with a financial planner before?" he asked.

"No, well, yes," Paul said. "Mack did say that they did have a current financial advisor. The last name was Sullivan, I believe, but I don't think he helped them with planning."

Larry wrote this on the board.

"Larry, do you think that maybe they had tried a do-it-yourself approach to planning?" Paul said.

"Can you really financially plan by yourself?" Larry said, thinking about this as he asked it. "Doesn't planning by definition require working with a professional?"

Planning, for Larry, was a tandem activity like dancing—

reciprocity and sharing were integrated into the process. Though many tried to go it alone, it was difficult. There were too many complex elements involved, such as taxes, investments, and insurance, along with goals and objectives, budgeting, and cash flow. Larry felt that professional training and an objective perspective were essential.

For both men, professional training came in the form of a certification in financial planning, which earned them the right to use the CFP® marks. Like a CPA or a licensed attorney, the CFP® certification is evidence of training in the technical fundamentals of financial planning, fulfilled by passing a series of rigorous exams, as well as completion of a minimum of three years of supervised fieldwork.

Larry sometimes referred to his method of planning as "Synoptic Financial Planning." He felt the word synoptic, which means "seeing things together," captured the essence of the discipline.

Through education, Larry and Paul fulfilled Principle 3, Competence, of the CFP Board Code of Ethics and Professional Responsibility, which required planners to attain and maintain "an adequate level of knowledge and skill, and application of that knowledge and skill in providing services to clients."

Paul finished going through his notes, telling Larry everything he remembered or knew about their new prospective clients. He also looked at Dr. Bell's website to get additional background information. "So, let's look at our agenda," Larry said, turning to Paul. "And we should try to get a copy out to the Bells today, please, ahead of the meeting."

"No problem," Paul said, checking to confirm that he had their email addresses.

Agenda

1. Getting to know you

    a. What activities do you like to do in your free time?

    b. What is your decision-making style? (For example: Quick? Slow?)

    c. What kinds of things do you value?

    d. What's important to you?

    e. What's your relationship like with your children? Parents? Siblings?

    f. Are you generally receptive to new ideas?

    g. Have you set goals in other parts of your life?

    h. What are some of your successes? Failures?

2. Explain the process of financial planning—five steps

    a. Gather facts.

    b. Analyze facts.

    c. Present plan.

    d. Implement Plan.

    e. Monitor plan.

3. Fact finding

    a. Go through fact finder conversationally.

        i. Document preliminary financial goals.

        ii. Begin to assess realistic time horizon for goals.

    b. Gather copies of investment statements, insurance policies, tax returns, and all other relevant information.

    c. Complete risk tolerance questionnaire.

4. Next steps

    a. Discuss expectations.

    b. Introduce Paul and other team members into the process.

"I assume," Larry said, "you'll send out the introductory letter to Dr. and Mrs. Bell that explains our process, introduces our team, etc.?"

"Yes," Paul said.

"As usual, I would like to get copies of all of their key documents so we can start to build their net worth statement," said Larry.

Since the Bells were new clients, with no direct connection to other clients, Larry would attend this first meeting without Paul. He felt it was difficult to build proper rapport with people when too many planners were on hand. Paul would be introduced into the plan at the second meeting if things went well.

Larry was sensitive to the fact that for many new clients, the process of planning felt overwhelming. He knew it was just as important to get to know people as it was to gather together all of the data. "OK," he said, "so I think we covered it all."

"Sounds good," Paul said, as he stood up to leave the conference room.

"Paul, let's not forget that every one of our financial plans begins with a relationship. Some sort of connection. We come together with clients because we can make a difference in their lives and because we care. That's it in a nutshell."

Paul smiled and nodded. "Thanks for the reminder, Larry. Now if you would please excuse me, I've got to go and get things ready for you. You'll be standing on their doorstep before you know it."

CHAPTER 5

Meeting Linda and Tom

Larry stood on the Bells' front porch and checked his watch. He had arrived on time. He rang the doorbell and took a deep breath. In the short interval of time before the door opened, he thought about how much he loved the start of a new plan. It always felt like a new adventure.

He heard footsteps, and Linda opened the door and greeted him with a friendly hello. She looked past Larry and said, "What a beautiful day!"

"Perfect conditions for financial planning—sunshine and blue skies overhead," Larry said, chuckling as he entered the home.

Linda laughed and said, "Well, don't be too sure, Mr. Morgan—you haven't seen our finances yet."

"Call me Larry, please."

Linda led him into the kitchen, where Tom was seated at the table. He stood up and greeted Larry with a handshake.

"Is this OK?" asked Linda, indicating the table.

"Perfect," Larry said, and handed Linda a box of oatmeal cookies. "These are fresh from a little place called McMillan's

Bakery in Haddon Township. I was there this morning and they brought these out as I was getting a cup of coffee.

"I know that place," said Linda as she opened the bag. "Mmmm, they smell delicious, thank you so much." She put the cookies on a plate and set them out in the center of the table.

"Can I get you a cup of coffee or tea?" she asked.

"Actually, a glass of water would be perfect," Larry said.

He sat down at the table. "You have a beautiful home," he said.

"Thanks," Linda said. "It was my parents' house originally, but we spruced it up a bit after we moved in. This property was a working farm originally."

Linda opened the blinds, revealing fields behind the house. She continued, "Although it's still run as a farm today, we don't work it ourselves. We lease the land to a farmer who grows corn for animal feed. The lease arrangement basically covers the cost of the real estate taxes on the land. Tom knows all of the details."

"Well, I really like it. My wife and I moved to Vineland from Mt. Laurel because of the farms. We love it here."

"Do you have any children?" asked Linda.

"Yes, three daughters," said Larry. He held up his cell phone and proudly flipped through a few pictures of the girls. "These are my angels," he said as he scanned through the pictures. Then Larry pointed to a picture of his wife, Melissa. "My wife's a social worker and we've been married for twenty-two years."

"Beautiful," said Linda. It was nice to get to know the personal side of their prospective financial planner, she thought to herself. "OK," she said, and then she took a deep breath. "So, where do we start?"

"Wherever you'd like," said Larry. He sensed Linda wanted to talk first. Without hesitation, she began discussing her concerns. She told the story about the bank balance running low and how they had never made it a point to save money, though she made it clear that she'd been brought up differently.

At this point, Tom rolled his eyes.

She said that her husband had a successful dental practice, but she expressed fear and remorse that so much time had been lost. Then came the part about the credit card balances and all of the loans. "I guess we have not been careful, and I'm worried," she said.

"About what?" asked Larry.

"Well," Linda said, "Tom's income has started slowing down. The insurance companies have not been paying like they used to, and frankly, we are both concerned about this."

"Can you tell me what are you worried about specifically?" asked Larry, leaning in.

"We're worried that we have no safety net," Linda said. "I feel like we have no security and no money for Tom to retire," Linda said.

"Your thoughts, Tom?" Larry asked, as he wrote Linda's points on his yellow pad.

Tom was sitting with his arms folded tightly over his chest. He thought for a moment then said, "I have to agree with my lovely wife, of course."

Larry smiled and looked at Linda, and then back at Tom. "Smart man," he said with a laugh.

"Stop it, Tom. Be serious," Linda scolded, as she gave Tom a playful knock on the shoulder.

"OK, OK," Tom said. His demeanor became serious, and he unfolded his arms. "No, really, I feel the same way. For years, we've been doing all kinds of things without restriction. We mostly buy things and travel, but we give money to charity, too, so don't think we spend only on ourselves. When you look over these papers you'll see some of that." Tom pointed to a stack of tax returns and bank statements he had brought to the table.

"The bottom line is that I can see that we need help," Tom said. "We have no plan. Our finances are all over the place. My number one concern is making sure that Linda is taken care of; if something should happen to me, I want her to be prepared."

"When you say that, what do you mean?" Larry said.

"If something should happen to the business," Tom said. "Like right now it's this insurance reimbursement thing. But I'm worried about other things too. Like, what if I were in an accident and couldn't work at all? Or what if I had a massive heart attack and died?"

"Oh, Tom!" gasped Linda.

"Well, I feel like we need to be prepared," Tom said. "Not having enough cash on hand is making me nervous as hell. To be honest, I just don't know where it all goes. I mean, I realize we spend it, but on what I don't know. It just goes. And it's the same with investing. Years ago, I invested $25,000 in some bio-tech stock thing that a friend told me was going to be huge. I can't even remember the name of it, but let's just say it went bust. That's our story."

Linda nodded.

The Bells then began talking about the kinds of values they'd been raised with, and what they were teaching their children when it came to finances. The more they talked about things, the more they began to feel a sense of relief.

As they spoke, Larry continued to write notes.

Eventually, Tom shared a goal that surprised Linda. "It's funny, but lately, I've been thinking about a day when I could retire from work. Sometimes I see flashes of it in my mind."

"Go on," Larry said.

"It hits me in weird places, in the office, or when I'm driving," Tom said.

"Really?" said Linda. Her voice was tender.

Tom nodded. "It's been on my mind lately, and it's true, I see myself taking more time off as I get older."

"Interesting," Larry said. As he leaned back in his chair he said, "Thank you both for sharing so much about yourselves."

"So, are we hopeless?" Tom said.

"Not at all. We can do this," Larry said with confidence. "Many people reach out to me and my firm at various points in time. When they sense something is not right, or when they're unsure of their next step, they often turn to us for help. What most people really need is a dedicated process to bring it all together. Financial planning is about approaching your finances one step at a time, and then applying this process. The secret is in the talking, like what we're doing here today. It's all about communicating."

Larry paused and watched as Tom and Linda seemed to take it all in. Then he continued, "Each time we meet, we'll approach different parts of your plan. You'll be amazed at how, over time, with each little step, the plan slowly comes together."

Larry knew that new planning relationships required effort

and care so trust could be built. There was, however, one additional critical element needed in order for the financial planning relationship to be successful—and that element was time. The passage of time was essential, which was a natural segue into a discussion of fees.

"The way we get paid to do this work," Larry said, "is that we charge a small percentage of assets that we manage and that you accumulate. You don't pay for any transaction fees."

Larry handed Tom and Linda a fee schedule.

"As you can see," he said, "when we manage assets of $1 million, our fee percentage is higher, but as assets grow through deposits and market performance, our fee percentage goes down. So with $5 million dollars' worth of assets under management, our fee percentage is 50 percent lower."

Larry explained that through this approach, the firm had a vested interest in the outcome. It was like a built-in reward and penalty system, so there was a constant focus on growing assets on the upside over time and preserving assets when markets were correcting. He also mentioned as well that the fee was fully disclosed on the first page of each quarterly performance report. He referred to this as full transparency.

"I never want to be in a fee dispute with anyone, and by doing it this way, it alleviates much of the mystery about how we get paid," Larry added.

"It makes sense to me," Tom responded. He liked that he did not have to write a check for the fee, and incur a direct new expense.

"Personally, Tom and Linda, what I also like about this approach is it enables me to align my interest with yours,"

Larry said. He went on to explain the distinction between this approach and the approach of brokers who sold investments and were paid commissions. With commissions, he felt there was a conflict of interest, as the financial advisor had to sell something to the client in order to generate a fee.

"Selling investments so I can profit through a commission is just not how I do it," Larry said. "It's not inherently wrong, but it doesn't fit my approach to wealth management. I want to live *inside* your plan."

Tom and Linda really appreciated hearing this. They told Larry they felt that this approach would work for them.

As Larry closed his notepad and placed it into his briefcase, he took a moment to do two very important things—say thank you and discuss next steps. A good planner is courteous first, and then always thinking ahead about what is coming next. "Linda, Tom, it has truly been a pleasure meeting you. Thank you for having me to your home and allowing me to spend time with you here." Larry patted the table.

"Here in good old Vineland," Tom added with a chuckle.

"Actually, not just here in Vineland," Larry said, "but right here, seated at your kitchen table."

"Oh, I see," Tom said and smiled.

"I like this place," Larry said. He followed the philosophy that financial planning meetings should be upbeat and easy-going. Though the topics were heavy, the aura should be light, which was necessary for nurturing the soul of the financial plan.

"As for next steps," Larry said, "I will be reviewing all of your information and sending you a summary letter that will outline the key points of our discussion. Then I will call you in about a week to check in, just to answer any follow-up questions you may have and see how you feel about proceeding forward." As he stood up, he added, "I think we are on the right track."

Tom and Linda both nodded and smiled.

Larry left the Bells' home with a good feeling in his heart—a warmth that comes from helping nice people find ways to reach their goals.

CHAPTER 6

Summary of Meeting

A day after the meeting, an email from Larry arrived in both Linda's and Tom's in-boxes.

Subject: Comprehensive Financial Planning Meeting

Dear Linda and Tom:

It was a pleasure having the opportunity to meet with you in your home to discuss your personal financial planning. I really enjoyed our thoughtful discussion. In this letter, I would like to provide you with a summary of our meeting and next steps, as follows:

In General. We spent the majority of our meeting talking about financial planning as well as process and structure. I shared with you how my firm and I approach the subject, including our team orientation, the meeting review process, and our approach to fees. At the end, I showed you some sample documents that we use in a typical financial planning engagement.

Goals. You shared several financial goals:

- To make certain Linda would be financially prepared in the event of a tragedy, like a death or disability event affecting Tom
- To get organized with all things financial
- To develop a strategy around savings and building wealth
- To implement strategies, where available, for saving on income taxes
- To adopt a proactive approach, as opposed to reactive
- To build enough wealth so that Tom has the option of slowing down at some point in the future and maybe retiring

Meeting Overview. Throughout our discussion, we talked about your resources, and you provided copies of all of your relevant documents. We also completed a risk tolerance questionnaire, which is a series of questions that help us ascertain the kind of risks you are comfortable taking in regard to your investments. Your profile indicated that you are comfortable with a balanced portfolio, equally focused on growth and income. We will discuss this profile in greater detail at our next meeting.

Next Steps. I will call you next week to see if you have any follow-up questions and to discern if you would like my firm to begin the process of preparing a more detailed financial plan for you.

Thank you for having me at your home and for taking the time to share so candidly your goals, concerns, and resources. I appreciate in advance the trust and confidence that you have placed in me.

Best regards.

Cordially,
Larry Morgan, CFP®

CHAPTER 7

Moving Forward

The following day, Larry received a call from Linda.

"After our meeting," she said, "Tom and I spoke and decided that we didn't want to wait until next week for you to call us. We want to get started today."

"That's good news," Larry said happily.

"We didn't want to delay this any longer. We feel like time is running out on us. To be perfectly honest, we're a little upset that we didn't seek help earlier."

"Linda, I've heard that said many times before, and what I can tell you is that once we begin and you see your plan come together, you'll feel a sense of confidence developing as we work together."

"Now that's something I can't wait to feel," Linda said with excitement in her voice.

Larry said that he needed copies of all recent account statements and other information they discussed at the meeting. Linda said she would get everything to him immediately.

"Joanne will call to schedule another meeting in two weeks," he told her, "and at that time I will present you with a complete financial plan. I'll also introduce my associate, Paul Hushingbuck, who will be working collaboratively with me. Eventually you will have a chance to meet our whole team."

As soon as he hung up the phone, Larry began thinking about how best to structure the upcoming meeting with the Bells. He jotted down some notes and began building his file.

Throughout the following week, he put the plan into the "steersman" of his mind's eye, ruminating and reflecting on the plan briefly every day. Though many planning ideas passed through his head, one nagging comment Tom had made weighed heavily. Tom said that for years he and Linda had been living a good life and spending without restriction. The idea of spending without any budgets or governance bothered Larry.

One morning, as Larry drove through the center of downtown Vineland on his way to work, he thought about ways the financial planning process could overcome excessive spending. His thoughts drifted back to his childhood. A vision appeared: He was six or seven years old and his mother was driving him to the local savings bank to make a deposit into his passbook savings account. In the car, his small hands held several rolls of pennies he had managed to collect over the preceding weeks. The night before, he and his mother sat together at the kitchen table painstakingly filling the penny rolls, and now they were on their way to make a deposit. Young Larry held a pliable blue passbook in his hand with his name typed on the inside cover. He flipped through the pages on the way to assess his previous progress, reviewing a growing balance—from $400, to $415, to $420, etc.

What he remembered most strongly was the feeling of pride that came each time he looked at his book. And after each deposit, he and his mother would leave the bank holding hands as they walked to the car. Larry sat in the back seat as they drove home, and reviewed his growing passbook balance again. He marveled at the interest that the bank credited to his account. When he asked his mother about the credited interest, she said, "It's the bank's way of saying thank you for letting them hold your money."

Larry smiled as he thought about this memory. He wanted to provide Linda and Tom with the same positive reinforcement about their savings plan as he'd had as a child. And then another thought came to him as he was pulling into the parking lot in front of his office.

The concept of savings, he realized, was nothing more than the byproduct of multiple episodes of delayed gratification. The interest that accrued in his childhood bank account, which was the positive reinforcement, came only after he had waited for a few weeks. Each time he gathered more pennies, rolled them, and took them to the bank to make the deposit, he would see his interest reward. It came through patience and leaving the savings to grow.

As a motivating idea for Linda and Tom, Larry decided he would buy them a ceramic piggy bank for the follow-up meeting. This would be a fun way to get them motivated. So he opened a search application on his phone and started searching.

Just as a shopping site was buffering, Larry's cell phone rang. Joanne was calling. She asked what time he would be arriving at the office and Larry told her he was already there in his car in the parking lot.

"Please hurry up," she said. "Paul and Barbara are here and want to review the Bells' financial plan with you. They said that there is a serious problem with it."

"No worries," Larry replied. "If it's their spending, please tell them I know, and have a plan."

As Larry hung up his phone, he looked to see if the search for the piggy bank had yielded any results.

Suddenly, he had an epiphany. Something he'd known for a while, but with the challenge of the Bells at hand, it became more apparent. Larry realized that we live in a culture of instant gratification. People have access to everything they could ever want to buy right in the palms of their hands via an Internet connection and a smartphone. Larry held up his phone and said to it, "How can I compete with you?"

The business of saving money meant saying no to buying some of the things people wanted. Linda and Tom would need to develop skills in the disciplined art of not spending money. Larry knew that through financial planning they would come to learn this over time.

He was not going to let that little phone with its big appeal get the better of his clients' plans. He placed his phone in his inside jacket pocket, and got out of the car. The process of setting goals around delayed gratification was the core biology of every good financial plan. This, plus positive support and encouragement, was how financial planners made assets magically appear.

CHAPTER 8

Arrival at the Office

"I've been thinking about the Bells' plan," Larry said as he walked into the conference room. Paul and Barbara looked up with blank expressions.

"What's that?" Paul said.

"I believe we need to positively support their savings. They need a reward for doing this."

"Listen, Larry, that's great, but we have bigger problems. Your meeting is in a few days and these projections just aren't working," Barbara said. There was frustration in her voice. "I can't get their assets to last for very long because their expenses are too high and the interest on all of their debt is eating up surpluses."

"That's what I was thinking about as well," Larry said. Barbara turned to the large television monitor on the wall that displayed the Bells' net worth statement.

Thomas and Linda Bell: Net Worth Statement

Assets:	Value:
Cash/Savings/CDs—3 Accounts	$35,000
Investments—6 Accounts	$250,000
IRA—Linda	$125,000
IRA—Tom	$145,000
Real Estate—Primary Residence	$780,000
Real Estate—Office	$250,000
Whole Life Insurance Cash Value	$24,000
Tom's Practice (Estimate)	$100,000
Total Assets	$1,709,000

Liabilities:	Value:
Credit Cards—11 Accounts	$89,000
Primary Mortgage	$465,000
Home Equity Line of Credit	$195,000
Car Loan	$14,000
Furniture Loan	$12,000
Real Estate Mortgage—Office	$150,000
Tom's Practice—Credit Outstanding	$112,000
Total Liabilities	$1,037,000

Total Assets	$1,709,000
Less: Total Liabilities	$1,037,000
Total Net Worth	$672,000

"Did you try running a higher return assumption?" asked Larry, hoping that maybe the Bells could take on more investment risk to solve the problem.

"I could do that," said Barbara, "but let's just say they would be taking on more risk than people should be taking at this stage in their lives, and more than the risk tolerance questionnaire indicated."

Paul reminded Larry that the couple had tested out as moderate investors, not aggressive.

"So guys, where does this leave us?" Larry said, as he sat back in his chair and removed his suit jacket.

"I think we know what the problem is . . . it's a classic case of overspending," said Barbara. "That's the bottom line. I mean, the debt service alone is more than $50,000 per year."

"So, now what?" Larry said.

The room became quiet as the team considered their options. At last, Paul spoke.

"We tell them the truth," he said in a flat, baritone voice.

Larry and Barbara looked over at him.

"I feel that we have a professional duty to tell them that they need to spend less or else they will be unable to reach their goals," Paul said. "It's really pretty simple."

"Then our meeting will be a reality check for them?" Larry said as both a statement and question.

"Absolutely," said Paul.

Larry nodded. "Guys," he said, "this is who we are and what we do. We are financial planners. We speak the truth."

"Yes," Paul said, sitting up straight.

Larry got up from his chair and walked over to the copy of the CFP Board Code of Ethics and Professional Responsibility that was hanging on the wall. He pointed at the document and read aloud: "Principle 2, Objectivity, 'requires intellectual honesty and impartiality.'"

Becoming a financial planner, for Larry, had been his calling. There was no giving up on anyone. In fact, he also believed that all people were capable of reaching goals. One of the tenets he lived by was that any goal, no matter how far out of reach it seemed, could be planned for.

"We should not give up on people just because we have a challenge ahead," he said, "and with these Bells, admittedly, the challenge is high. But we will tell them the truth."

He stood up and walked over to the window. As he stared at the trees that flanked the parking lot, he thought about Tom and Linda's future. They had plans and fears just like everyone else. They simply desired to get their financial life under control. "Guys, there is really a great responsibility in the work we do," he said turning away from the window. "As financial planners, we are serving a very important need."

He sat back at the table. "I think the Bells are aware of their spending issues. When I sat down with them, Linda made it obvious that she knew things were not OK. They were scared, and that's exactly why we're needed. Where some other financial planners might only help if the clients' accounts were bigger or if they'd been better savers, we're different. We won't walk away from this challenge, but instead, we'll walk alongside and help them. Tom has a good practice and they are nice people. Let's help them embrace delayed gratification, and when surpluses start to build, we'll catch them and set them aside."

Paul and Barbara exchanged glances and nodded.

"Their confidence will grow as time progresses and their rewards begin to build," Larry said. "It's brilliant. That's a plan."

CHAPTER 9

Presenting the Financial Plan

A financial plan has a certain lifelike quality to it. It inhales when markets fluctuate, and exhales when personal circumstances change. Plan preparations are made, then altered, then repeatedly reconfigured.

By the time Larry and Paul were seated with Linda and Tom at their kitchen table, they had a plan. Their main goal was to help Tom and Linda pursue their goal of becoming financially confident, along with the gradual goal of allowing Tom to retire from the practice of dentistry.

Using a portable display screen connected to a laptop, Larry and Paul went over various charts and graphs explaining their plan. They began by going over their net worth statement.

"Unbelievable," Linda said. She shook her head as she gazed over the figures. "I had no idea our credit card bills had gotten so high."

Tom looked on with disbelief as well, adding, "Sheesh, look at my practice value."

"Well," Larry said, "let's bear in mind that we're only making an estimate of the value of your practice. It could be worth more, but we would need to ask Mack."

As Larry went through their assets one by one, line by line, Linda and Tom added comments. Larry listened carefully. There were positive factors, like the fact that they had managed to commit to IRAs for a number of years, and that they had an investment account with several holdings in it. Larry had performed a review of these assets and stated that their financial advisor, Mr. Sullivan, had done a decent job in adding securities. He pointed out that there was a difference between a financial advisor who manages a portfolio without connecting it to any plan, versus a planner who does both.

When he went through the liabilities, though, it was a different story. As he spoke, Linda and Tom began to writhe, as if they were in pain. They were seeing for the first time the effect of the years of accumulated debt upon their asset base. It was hard for them to hear that without the debts, their net worth was nearly $1.5 million and with the debt nearly $1 million less.

Linda was really shaken by this, and at one point, Tom put his arm around his wife. But it was of little use. She shrugged away his advance and leaned toward the computer to study more closely the debt items line by line.

Among the most shocking visuals for the couple were the graphs depicting the future of their finances in the absence of a plan. A blue bar represented their liquid net worth and a gold bar ran on top of it, representing their life expectancies. With no planning, their resources would be depleted well before the end of their lives.

There were other alarming graphs, like the one that showed Tom dying prematurely. Once again, the blue bar ended only a few years following his passing, depicting the exhaustion of their resources.

At one point, Linda pointed to the lines on the screen, and asked in a quivery voice, "So will I be here . . . alone, with no assets . . . nothing in the bank?"

Larry calmly confirmed that she was correct. He knew that when clients saw these kinds of scenarios for the first time, it was important to move very slowly. In many instances, the questions came in the form of trying to better understand the information. This was a typical part of the process.

"What's this?" Linda said, pointing to the screen.

"This graph shows the effect of Tom developing Alzheimer's disease five years from now. I assumed this scenario with a savings plan, but without a long-term care plan."

Larry went on to tell them about a client who experienced a similar scenario. His income ceased and custodial nursing care was needed at a cost of $90,000 per year.

The Bells looked at the chart, then at each other, and then back to the chart.

"The declining line here represents a spending down of the resources you'd managed to save over the first five years before the Alzheimer's set in," Larry said. "Here you see Linda has kept the house, but the savings goes like this." He pointed to the blue line, which faded away.

Linda looked visibly rattled.

Larry and Paul used conservative assumptions to depict all of their projections, such as inflation remaining at historical averages, and market returns keeping consistent with averages from the past twenty years. They also assumed life expectancies would continue through age one hundred, though there was some soft questioning from Tom about whether living to one hundred was realistic.

Linda shared that her father had died at age eighty-one, but her mother was still alive and living independently at eighty-seven.

"You have good genes," Larry responded.

Tom added that his parents had died together in a tragic automobile accident only a few years before. They had both been in their seventies.

Larry said he used the age of one hundred for estimating life expectancies. His orientation was to be conservative, which the Bells agreed was best.

Given the Bells' obvious shock, especially on the point of long-term care, Larry briefly mentioned that a death event would cause the same rapid depletion. He also noted that their modest life insurance would extend resources, though only slightly.

Larry wrapped up the no-planning "Present Scenarios" portion.

"In the absence of planning, you will likely run out of assets relatively rapidly with any life change, whether it is Tom retiring, dying, or becoming disabled. Your goal," he said, looking at Tom, "of caring for Linda would not be accomplished."

Larry paused, waiting for Linda and Tom to process the reality of this last statement.

"OK," Linda said at last. "Let me just say that this looks terrible. I mean, really, my fears were justified. If we don't start saving our money now, we could be in big trouble later, right?"

"Correct."

She blew her nose into a tissue as Tom continued staring at the laptop display. "I feel the same way as Linda," he said at last. "This is a real eye-opener."

Tom paused; he seemed to be struggling to find his next words. "I had a feeling something was off, but now I can see that I will never retire, and if I ever had to stop working for some reason, Linda and I can forget about everything."

Larry sat quietly. Tom stared at the screen again. Larry knew that seeing the future without a financial plan was often a catalyst to making changes. He'd heard it said about planning that people only make a change when they feel the heat or see the light; Linda and Tom were definitely feeling and seeing both.

"So," Larry said, "financial planners look at these unplanned scenarios. We think and find ways to best address them, and we do so with 'honesty and candor which must not be subordinated to personal gain and advantage.' This is Principle 1, Integrity, of the CFP Board Code of Ethics," he said, pointing to the dwindling blue lines.

It was time to launch the antidote for this dire potential outcome—the plan itself.

Methodically, he took the Bells through a five-point plan that included a lifestyle budget to control spending, a personal savings strategy, an emergency plan, a plan for managing unexpected catastrophes like chronic illness or death, and a plan to help Tom gradually get to retirement. The charts and graphs that illustrated this possibility showed longer blue lines.

"So, we can make this work," Larry said. "But make no mistake about it—it will take effort. We have to get a budget together and stick to it. The budget is our most important starting place, and Paul will meet with you later to create one that will work for you. Once you have this and implement it, we will track it. I fully expect that you will have surpluses."

Tom was nodding.

Paul displayed a new chart on the screen.

"Your dental practice will become our engine," Larry said. His voice was clear and confident. "We will use it to build resources."

The first step Larry described was the development of an emergency fund. The Bells would need to set aside at least six months' worth of expenses in a cash account to cover an emergency, he explained. Once that was in place, a savings and debt repayment plan could begin.

For savings, he recommended a 401(k) profit-sharing plan at the dental office, explaining how it would be designed to benefit older employees. The plan would be a way to make savings easier for Tom as the savings deposits would be tax deductible as a business expense. Likewise, other staff members would be able to deposit small amounts of their pay each week and get tax deductions as they, too, saved for retirement.

Tom and Linda nodded in agreement.

"As for the debts," Larry said, "we will start with the highest rates first and begin paying back a little bit each month."

"OK," Tom said.

"Finally, we need to address contingencies. We need a plan in case something happens to you, Tom."

"You mean insurance, right?"

"Yes, insurance." Larry diagramed various approaches that would work, using different types, such as life insurance and long-term care insurance. He also noted that a property and auto insurance review was needed.

Larry went back to the computer display. This time, Paul brought up a chart with the heading "With Financial Plan." This projection showed that with a financial plan, the Bells' resources could be made to last through their life expectancies, with Tom eventually slowing down and retiring from his practice.

"You can do this," Larry said. "I know you can."

Tom and Linda exhaled simultaneously, then laughed. It was obvious that they fully understood their predicament.

Larry shared a story about other clients, a couple who were in a similar state ten years before, with very little saved and with large debts. They owned a good business with steady cash flow, but had no financial plan. "Through careful planning and review, this couple has now managed to save more than $1.5 million," Larry said enthusiastically. "They are still debt-free and going strong."

Linda and Tom exchanged excited looks.

"I believe by working together on a plan, it will succeed," Larry said. "That goals, all goals, when undertaken with a team, and written down and monitored regularly, are possible and achievable."

He began to gather his papers. "Now you know a little bit about Larry Morgan. He's a guy who believes in reaching goals and getting things done. That's me."

Larry stood up, and Paul followed his lead. They put the papers into their briefcases and Larry said, "A meeting summary letter will come soon, and it will include next steps. Then, I will call you in about a week or so to check in and see if you feel ready to implement this plan."

Linda told him that she'd shared the financial planning news with her mother, who had been very happy to hear about it. "'I raised a saver, not a spender,'" Linda said, imitating her mother's Russian accent and waving her forefinger at Larry.

As Tom and Linda walked Paul and Larry to the door, Larry assured them that everything would work out well. Then he reached into his pocket. "I almost forgot, I got you a little present."

He handed them a small pink ceramic piggy bank.

"This will serve as a reminder to save more," said Larry. Tom and Linda laughed.

On the doorstep, he turned to them and said, "I know it's hard to believe at this early stage, but I will let you in on a little secret. Over time, through review meetings and revisiting goals and progress, you will come to see that there is a life that lives inside your financial plan. It's an actual soul. Right now, it's non-existent, but one day, take my word for it, it will happen. You will know when the soul of your plan is there. It's amazing."

Linda smiled. "OK Larry, if you say so."

As Larry started to walk down the porch steps, he missed a step. Paul caught him just as he was falling.

"Larry, are you OK?" Linda gasped.

"I'm fine," he said, looking back at the row of steps. "Nice catch, Paul."

When the door closed, Linda held the little bank in her hand and hugged Tom tightly. Then she looked into his eyes, and felt a sense of closeness and excitement—similar to the way she felt after that first meeting. Linda was glad she and Tom were embarking on this journey together.

PART TWO

The Financial Plan Implementation

CHAPTER 10

Meeting Follow-Up

The day after the meeting, Larry emailed a summary letter to Tom and Linda.

Subject: Financial Planning Meeting

Dear Linda and Tom:

It was a pleasure to meet with you at your home to discuss financial planning. In this letter, I would like to outline our discussion and next steps, as follows:

1. **General Update:** We chatted briefly about your family, and we really enjoyed hearing about your grandchildren. Also, one day we look forward to meeting your daughter, Jessica, and son, Greg.

2. **Financial Plan Overview:** We spent the bulk of our meeting going through your financial plan. We reviewed your net worth statement and projected cash flow report. Our goal was to simulate your future based upon no financial plan versus implementing a financial plan. We looked at the kind of resources that would be necessary

to accomplish one of your main financial goals, Tom's eventual slowdown from the practice of dentistry. We used conservative projections throughout our models. The results indicated that in the absence of a financial plan, it appeared that you would be unable to build a sustainable base from which to generate future income. With planning, the results indicated a more appealing picture, one that demonstrated that surpluses could be captured from your cash flow and be used to fund a savings base that would generate income at a later time. As part of your plan, we are recommending:

- Implementation of a 401(k) profit-sharing retirement plan at Tom's office
- Implementation of professionally managed, asset-allocated portfolios
- Implementation of proper insurance—life, long-term disability, long-term care, and a property & casualty insurance review
- Implementation of an emergency fund
- Implementation of a debt-reduction program
- Implementation of a budget, along with a tracking and electronic bill paying system for expenses

3. **Next Steps.** I will call you next week to see if you have any questions and are ready to implement your plan. If you are agreeable to moving forward, Paul and I will need to develop an implementation plan. This is a formal plan that will help us properly time-line all of the above. There

is much to do and our goal is to make certain that the process does not feel overwhelming.

Thank you for allowing us to put all of this together for you. We appreciate the trust and confidence that you have placed in us and look forward to speaking to you soon.

Best Regards.

Cordially,

Larry Morgan, CFP®

cc: Paul Hushingbuck, Barbara Foster, and Joanne McGlaughlin

CHAPTER 11

Decisions

When Linda received the email summary letter from Larry on her phone, she read it and right away called Tom at work.

"Hi, honey," she said, "sorry to bother you, but we were both emailed Larry's letter. I just read it, and I think everything looks good. Are you OK if I tell him to move forward with our plan?"

Tom said, "Go for it. We should've done this years ago."

Linda then called Larry and said, "Larry, we're ready. Let's get going with our plan while we still have some time." And she laughed.

Larry said, "That's great news. Did you have any questions?"

Linda thought for a moment and said, "My only question is how quickly can we get everything into place?"

"It'll take a little bit of time for us to prepare everything, but once papers are signed things move pretty fast."

Linda sounded confident and optimistic, a far cry from the woman who'd initially contacted him. Once again, Larry marveled at the sheer power that lay at the core of getting goals down on paper, assembling a team, and organizing resources and a process.

"Linda," he said, "Paul and I will meet up in the next day or so to put together a detailed implementation plan. We should meet again next week to go over the details. Some aspects are quick, but others take time. When we meet, we will go through the time frame around each part."

"Great. Larry, we're really ready. Just let us know what we need to do. You have two very motivated clients."

When Larry hung up the phone, he called Paul. "My friend," he said, "the time has come. Let's plan the start of the plan."

CHAPTER 12

The Implementation Plan

An implementation plan is a functional and important part of the planning process. It basically consists of an ordering of the plan and step-by-step documentation of the plan timeline. When Larry heard the words "let's begin" from a prospective client, it was time to call a meeting in the conference room with the entire financial planning team—Paul, Barbara, and Joanne.

"So, it looks like Tom and Linda are ready to move forward," Barbara said with enthusiasm.

The start of a new plan is a time of excitement as well as trepidation. The excitement comes from having a new relationship, but the trepidation comes from all of the little details that must be taken care of. There are many procedural aspects at the start of every plan that have to be considered, such as unexpected fees that can be levied when accounts are moved, taxes incurred when old assets are sold, and potential underwriting issues that may arise when new insurance is involved.

Then there is the paperwork. Each account requires forms of all sorts—forms for opening accounts, forms for moving accounts, forms for designating beneficiaries, etc. The process has to be organized. Larry had learned over time that you cannot rush a plan's implementation. It's in haste to begin that mistakes can be made.

"Ladies," he said, with a nod to Joanne and Barbara, "and gentleman . . . I present to you, Linda and Tom Bell, our newest clients."

Larry held up the file and opened it. With a feeling of humble gratitude, he handed out copies of the initial meeting letter and the financial plan summary letter. He was grateful to have found people to help who were appreciative and nice.

Over the years, Larry had come to learn that although not all clients were the same, the one attribute they all shared was the need for ongoing communication with clearly expressed expectations set at the start. It was on this point that the firm would make its first impression. "Let's look together at their goals and how we designed the plan," he said to his team.

Paul, Barbara, and Larry then discussed all aspects of the Bells' situation. They talked about both short-term goals, like budgeting and cash flow, and long-term plans to increase savings. They also discussed the goal of making sure Linda was prepared if something should happen to her husband.

They then went over the new account setup and the consolidation and movement of the old accounts. Finally, they considered setup of a new retirement plan at Tom's practice. They decided it would be best to follow this order:

1. Implement new investment accounts and the rollover of existing assets.

2. Work on the budgeting and cash flow.

3. Begin a retirement plan.

4. Prepare insurance options.

5. Establish a quarterly-review meeting schedule.

"I think that this implementation plan makes sense," Larry said. "I will draft a letter to the Bells outlining the plan." And then he paused, and looked at one of their current account statements. "You know, guys, I do think about Tom and Linda's former advisor, Wayne Sullivan. I don't know Mr. Sullivan, nor can I tell you why he never invested time in helping the Bells connect their asset accumulation to their financial goals and objectives."

Paul said, "Maybe he wasn't a planner?"

"That might be true," Barbara said. "Very few advisors think about the 'what if?' scenarios we planners spend so much time on."

"You know, covering every aspect is what comprehensive financial planning is really about," Larry said, "but it still gives me pause to think about Mr. Sullivan. He did a decent job of helping them get to this point. But who knows? Maybe he just didn't believe there was more that could be done here. Maybe he saw their spending habits and got scared."

"Well, Larry, you earned the opportunity to help these people," Barbara said. "I wouldn't worry too much about their former advisor."

Larry said, "Actually, I do worry—I worry about his practice, his wife and kids, his goal of making a living just like the rest of us. Maybe we don't know Mr. Wayne Sullivan, but in many ways he is just like us."

Larry then said he'd call Linda and Tom and tell them it was customary and proper courtesy to call an advisor before an account was moved, and would coach them on the proper things to say and how to handle it.

"If I were to lose a client," Larry said, "I would want to receive a call from my client. I know it may be upsetting, but that's how I'd want to be treated."

Larry followed the Golden Rule of treating others in the same way he wanted to be treated. This was Principle 4, Fairness, of the CFP Board Code of Ethics. Larry exemplified this aspect in all of his dealings with people.

In fact, he approached every aspect of his life through the lens of treating people respectfully and with a sense of doing what was right.

CHAPTER 13

An Unplanned Occurrence

On the day Larry and Paul were scheduled for a follow-up meeting with the Bells, Linda received an unexpected call. It was from a friend of her mother's who sounded very upset.

"Oh dear, your mother collapsed unexpectedly during our bridge game. We called an ambulance. They picked her up and took her to the hospital. I'm worried about her. You need to go to the hospital right away. She's at Vineland Main."

In shock, Linda immediately called Tom at work to tell him she was heading to the hospital and why. Tom said he would meet her there.

She also quickly tapped a text message to Larry. "Sorry—need to reschedule our meeting today. Emergency. Mom rushed to hospital. Heading to Vineland Main."

Linda pressed "send," then grabbed her pocketbook and left her home quickly.

As she pulled into the parking lot of the hospital, a vision flashed before her eyes. She had liked to play dress-up with her mother's clothes when she was a little girl, often wearing her mother's oversized shoes and dresses that hung down to her feet. She paraded around the house with her dolls, pretending that she was a mother taking care of her babies. Linda turned off her car. She realized that she needed to care for her mother now; it was her time to be the caregiver.

Once inside, the receptionist directed her to the Intensive Care Unit, where she was met by the emergency room attending physician. He delivered somber news. Her mother was not doing well. She had suffered a stroke and banged her head fairly hard on the floor when she fell. The full extent of the damage was unknown, but at this time her vitals were stable and she was resting. Linda's training as a nurse had not prepared her for this moment. Now, for the first time ever, she would need to be the one to care for her mother—the woman who had always been a symbol of strength and independence. Linda only briefly saw her mother, who was lying in a bed with her eyes closed, before a male nurse dressed in blue scrubs directed her to the waiting room.

When she entered the waiting room, a woman was sitting there with a despondent look on her face. She handed Linda a few tissues, and Linda politely said thank you. Tom arrived within the hour and the two of them spent the remainder of the afternoon worried and nervous, seated among other worried and nervous people. At 4:50 p.m., after several hours, someone familiar arrived in the waiting area. It was Larry Morgan. He gave Linda a warm hug, shook Tom's hand, and then sat down.

Larry asked about Linda's mother, genuinely interested in learning more about her and what had happened. Linda explained her disbelief that this was happening; the stroke . . . the fall . . . the injury to her head. She shared her fears and the uncertainty of what would happen next.

She also shared stories about her mother, telling Larry how she'd immigrated to America and had taught Linda the meaning of a dollar. How she had encouraged Linda and her sister to go to college.

Tom told him that Helen made sure the family was always protected. "Sometimes, she could be a little overly protective," he said, "but she is really a selfless person. No question about it."

After an hour or so, Larry looked at his watch and said he had to get going.

"Larry, before you go, I have a question," Linda said. "I'm not sure if this is the proper time, but well, it's about my mother's situation."

"Of course," Larry said.

"The doctor said that based on her age and the extent of bruising on her frail body from the fall, she will likely need rehabilitation. He wasn't sure for how long, but it could be for a long time. I mean, look, she's almost ninety years old. I should be ready for the reality that she may need to be placed in a rehab facility or nursing home."

As she said this, her voice quivered, and her eyes started tearing up. Tom handed her a tissue.

"I mean," she said with a sob, "we don't know how long it's going to be. What should we be doing?"

With a quiet voice, Larry said, "The first thing that comes to mind is whether your mother has a signed power of attorney document."

"Yes, I have a copy of it back at the house," Linda said. "I've got copies of all of her estate planning documents."

"Very good. That's the first step. Let's get those in hand," said Larry.

"Mom was a planner. She took care of these things a long time ago," Linda said.

Larry explained that the estate planning documents should all be reviewed, but the process of planning really required a better understanding of Helen's financial resources along with an understanding of the expected cost of care. Facility care was expensive and Larry pointed out that resources often played a part in the decision-making process. At the hospital, a social worker would soon be appointed to help go over the options, but they might or might not be what Helen would have wanted.

"What do you mean?" asked Linda.

"Well, as you can guess, what happens is that the social worker will do her best to find an opening for your mother at a nursing facility, but there are higher-end nursing homes and then there are others. You really need to see for yourself so you can make an informed decision."

"So, should we tour the local facilities tomorrow?" asked Tom.

"I think the sooner you do that, the better, just to be safe," said Larry.

"I know you have your hands full with us, but I could really use your help with going over—"

But before Linda could finish, Larry said that he would be happy to help out. As he got up to leave, the Bells' children entered the waiting room area. Linda introduced Larry to Jessica and Greg.

As Larry turned to leave, Linda grabbed his arm and looked

him square in the eye. "I will not," she said, "have my mother go to any nursing facility for longer than needed. I promised her years ago that if anything ever happened like this, she was not going to one."

Tom put his arm around his wife to steady her.

"Linda, don't worry," Larry said. "We will go through things and figure it out. I'll ask Joanne to clear some time for us to meet as soon as possible. We can even meet at your mother's home."

Linda nodded gratefully. "Even with care in the home, I don't know if I could trust anyone with Mom," she said, and Tom nodded in agreement.

Larry assured them that by sitting down and getting organized, the process typically assured that the right decision would become evident. "Oh, by the way," he added, "I will send over a letter summarizing your implementation plan. The one that Paul and I put together for you for today's meeting. We'll reschedule our appointment once things settle down, but at least you will have the implementation plan in hand."

On Larry's drive home, he thought about what Linda had said about the fact that Mrs. Drusselovsky had her estate planning documents all ready. He wondered what had driven Helen to do this. How did a woman who was an immigrant to this country and spoke little English know how to be so prepared?

Linda had shared the story about the ship that brought Helen from Russia to America along with her parents and other family members. Helen's mother did not survive the journey. Helen had probably been conditioned to always prepare for the unexpected. As a result, she intuitively knew to plan, to be prepared for whatever situations might be ahead. This was part of her immigrant story. So many people arrived in America without a plan but learned to be ready and prepared.

She lived with the spirit of financial planning in her heart— by organizing her life and affairs in preparation for what was *likely* to happen, *could possibly* happen, or *would* happen.

CHAPTER 14

The Next Day

At the office the next morning, Larry was greeted by his assistant, Joanne. He spoke with her about Mrs. Drusselovsky's sudden turn and his visit with Tom and Linda at the hospital.

"It feels good to be part of an organization that not only cares about its clients, but one that actually shows it . . . I love that! You rock, Morgan," Joanne said.

"We need to be there for our clients in their time of need," said Larry. "We can't just look over their data and ruminate about their future. The most important things happen in real time. In the present moment."

"Yes, I can see that," said Joanne with a nod.

"Speaking of the here and now, what is our day looking like?" Larry asked, as he perused the files that were beginning to pile up on his desk.

Joanne explained that he had clients in the morning and afternoon, plus he'd received a call from Peggy Abramowitz. "Apparently, she'd heard about Linda's mother and wanted to know if we could squeeze her in sometime today to talk about her own long-term care planning. She sounded worried, so I told her to come in late this afternoon," Joanne said.

"You know," Larry said, "I never say when it rains, it pours."

"Really," said Joanne with a smile, "Why's that?"

"Because it never rains, it only pours."

"You got that right," laughed Joanne, as she headed back to her desk.

Larry told Joanne he needed to schedule a meeting with Linda to go over her mother's finances as soon as possible. He then sat down at his desk and drafted an email to Linda summarizing his firm's implementation plan for her and Tom.

Despite the setback with Helen, he was determined to get Linda and Tom's financial plan off the ground.

CHAPTER 15

Linda and Larry
Review Helen's Finances

Over the next two weeks, Linda traveled frequently back and forth from the hospital. There were many meetings with doctors and physical therapists, along with speech and occupational therapists. Her primary focus had been to get her mother well enough so that she could be discharged from the hospital and recuperate at her home. The whole process was enormously stressful. On the morning that her mother was having a cognitive assessment completed, Linda was able to find time to meet with Larry.

"So, here we are, we can finally do this," Linda said with a deep breath as she sat down with Larry in the kitchen of her mother's townhouse.

"This is a nice place," said Larry, looking around.

"My mother moved in here about twelve years ago. Most of the people that live here are either her age, or a bit younger, but all live independently."

"I see."

"I would say that overall, she's been happy here. I've got to get her back here soon. A hospital is no place to live."

"Agreed," said Larry.

"So, where do we start?" Linda said.

Larry recommended that she begin meeting with home care agencies so she could have her options lined up when the time came.

Linda told Larry that she hadn't gotten around to looking at nursing homes as he had suggested. "I just couldn't bear the thought of Mom going into a home. It was too difficult to think about," Linda said.

"Let's take a look at her resources, as it will give us an idea of her options," Larry said, and then he went to work. He reviewed account statements, bills, and Helen's checkbook. He input all of the key values in his laptop computer, and then, after reviewing his work, he said, "Here is our starting place, your mother's net worth statement."

Helen Drusselovsky's Net Worth Statement

Assets:	Value:
Cash/Checking/Savings at 5 Banks	$150,000
CDs—36; 6 Different Banks	$415,000
Fixed Annuities—8 Accounts	$585,000
Individual Stocks (Blue Chips/Utilities)	$365,000
Treasury Bonds	$170,000
US Savings Bonds—I & EE Bonds	$135,000
Municipal Bonds	$250,000
Primary Residence	$200,000
Total Assets	**$2,270,000**
Less: Total Liabilities	**$0**
Total Net Worth	**$2,270,000**

"Your mother was really a great saver," said Larry, as he perused the finished report with her.

Linda said, "Now you see, Larry, why I am so motivated to get on the right track. This is what I was talking about. This is how I was raised."

The process she was going through because of her mother's stroke was very emotional, but seeing her mother's resources, even before Larry gave his impression, brought her tremendous comfort. It seemed as though her mother had been planning for this very moment. Like she was saving for an emergency.

"I can tell a lot about your mother from looking at her finances," Larry said. "The first thing is that she didn't trust banks, as she has multiple accounts at different ones."

"That must be a holdover from Russia," Linda said. "Maybe from when she was a girl? Her parents went through the Great Depression, so maybe that had something to do with it."

"Makes sense," Larry said. "The next thing that's clear to me is that she was a very safe investor. She bought mostly things that had guarantees, like fixed deferred annuities, which had guarantees based on the claims-paying ability of the issuing company. And then there are these stocks," Larry said as he pointed to the computer screen, "but even these are defensive and relatively low risk. All with great companies."

"So, this looks good to you?" Linda said.

"Yes," he replied. "Your mother has resources, which means she has options. When it comes time for her to leave the hospital, this'll make it easier for you to decide on the best option. We don't know the cost of things yet, but we will."

"What a relief," Linda said, and smiled. "Thanks, Larry."

Larry was happy to review Linda's mother's information. It was helpful for Linda and Tom's plan as well, for it denoted resources that might come to Linda as a future inheritance. Larry did not raise this aspect, however, as it was unnecessary and could become emotional.

"Now, for you and Tom," he said. "Do you want to try and schedule time to go over your implementation plan? Did you get my summary letter? There's no rush on my end, I just want to make sure I keep it moving forward."

Larry spoke in a gentle manner. He understood that Linda's primary focus was her mother.

"I have it," Linda said, "but have not had a chance to read it. However, Tom and I are going on a day trip this weekend to Longwood Gardens, and I'm bringing your letter with us to go over it on our drive. I'll call you next week."

"Sounds good," Larry said. "I've never been there before, but I've heard it's beautiful. I'm glad to hear you're taking a little time for yourself. I know it's been a long couple of weeks for you."

They collected Helen's papers and left them in a neat pile on the table. They also reviewed her power of attorney, which named Linda as attorney-in-fact. Larry pointed out that with this document and the net worth statement, Linda would be ready when the time came to meet with the social worker who would likely handle the discharge and go over her mother's plan of care.

After a final thank you, they parted. Linda was ready for a break.

CHAPTER 16

Longwood Gardens

In the past, a vacation meant a week of travel to Europe, fine dining, and shopping, but in the spirit of building their nest egg, Linda and Tom decided to simply take a day trip to Longwood Gardens, a beautiful four-hundred-acre park located just outside of Philadelphia.

Their visit took place during the park's annual Chrysanthemum Festival. They strolled the floral grounds, and learned about its benefactor, Pierre S. du Pont. The admission to the garden was $27 per person, and they stopped for dinner on the way home at a small Italian restaurant. The cost for dinner was $46 including tip. The total cost for the day was exactly $100.

For Linda and Tom, this trip was a rite of passage. Though they did indeed need a break, it was imperative to Linda that they evidence a commitment to their personal financial plan. She had wanted to put a savings plan into action since their first meeting with Larry; however, with her mother's stroke, she was forced to put things temporarily on hold.

As Tom and Linda drove back to Vineland, they were reflective.

"Well, we did it," said Linda, looking at Tom with a smile.

"Yes, we did. It was a wonderful day and it cost us next to nothing. I loved that Lookout Loft . . . just loved it," said Tom excitedly.

They drove in contented silence for a while. "Honey, when do we see Larry next?" Tom said.

"I think he suggested in about two weeks."

"I'm thinking about the retirement plan he mentioned—you know, the 401(k) plan for my office. I think it's a good idea. I think we should get that going."

"Really?" Linda said with pleasant surprise, looking over at Tom.

"We managed to enjoy ourselves today without spending a fortune. And that got me thinking about the money we're probably saving. Maybe it can go into a retirement plan of some sort."

Tom was revealing a new side that Linda was quite happy to see. It was becoming clear that avoiding expensive activities was like any other change activity—dieting, fitness, or a new hobby. The common thread was personal commitment. Their commitment was sacrificing spending today in order to generate savings for tomorrow.

"So, what's next?" Tom said.

"We gave Larry the go-ahead, and he sent us a letter, which I just happen to have right here . . ." Linda said as she rummaged through her pocketbook and pulled out a folded piece of paper. She waved it in the air. And then she read it out loud.

Dear Tom and Linda:

My team and I are sorry to hear about Linda's mother, Helen. Please know that she is in our thoughts and prayers for a speedy recovery.

Also, I am sorry that we did not have time to meet recently to implement your financial plan. With regard to your planning, thank you for giving us the opportunity and privilege of helping you work toward your financial goals. We appreciate the trust and confidence that you have placed in our firm.

Since we did not meet, I wanted to outline for you the steps that make up the implementation phase of your financial plan. These are as follows:

Establishing New Accounts. Setting up your investment accounts is critical so that we can begin implementing the savings strategies that we discussed. Furthermore, we want to consolidate several duplicative accounts so as to make the oversight of your investment portfolio more efficient. Your new portfolio for your various accounts will be significantly different than your present one in that it will follow principles of asset allocation and diversification. This means we will need to sell most of your existing positions and replace them with new positions. Tax implications will be considered and communicated throughout the process and we will touch base with your tax advisor, Mack Fletcher, before we do anything. All new positions will be overseen by our firm's investment committee, headed by Barbara Foster. We meet weekly to discuss the economy, along with the investment positions we have selected. We will prepare the necessary New Account forms to begin the process and Joanne will schedule a time to get together to sign them. (Paul/Barbara/Joanne)

**There is no guarantee that a diversified portfolio will enhance overall returns or outperform a non-diversified portfolio. Diversification and asset allocation do not protect against market risk.

Retirement Planning. One of the centerpieces of your financial plan is the implementation of a 401(k) profit-sharing plan at Tom's practice. This plan will create a valuable income tax deduction from Tom's practice income, which will make retirement savings more efficient. The idea is to deduct the contribution today while you are in a high tax bracket, grow assets in a tax-deferred environment, and then make distributions at the time of retirement, when you are in a lower tax bracket. I feel that this will be a perfect way to jumpstart your plan, with an eye toward our first goal of providing Tom with the means to slow down. I will ask Joanne to arrange for us to speak with a pension administrator to talk about designing a plan. Like the way we set up new accounts, there will be forms and documents to implement. (Joanne/Larry)

Insurance Planning. We have some work to do around putting in place the proper insurance. This includes planning for three types of catastrophes—a loss of income should Tom become sick or have an accident; a loss of income to Linda if Tom were to pass away; and finally, a catastrophe involving a property loss or exposure to a liability like a lawsuit. I want to make sure we have properly covered all of these contingencies, as any one of them could negatively impact the outcome of your plan. Once we have put together some options for you, Joanne will schedule a meeting so we can go over managing these risks. (Larry/Barbara/Joanne)

** Please note that unlike the investment oversight, for which we charge an asset-management fee, there is no fee related to insurance planning. Rather, the insurance companies pay licensed agents a commission set by the carriers, which is embedded in the cost of the coverage.

Budget. A budget is necessary to help you get a better handle on your spending. It was beneficial for us to understand how you are spending so we can look for ways to find surpluses that can be set aside for savings. We want to work with you to get a reasonable budget together and also to automate the process of keeping track of expenses. Paul will make a date with you to begin the process of documenting expenses and reviewing systems for automation. (Paul)

Monitoring Progress. Once we have concluded the initial phases of our implementation, we will be ready to set up a regular review meeting schedule. The review meetings are essential, as they give us the opportunity to update the plan for any changes, to monitor the progress you are making toward reaching your goals, and most importantly, to designate time for communicating. Our scheduling coordinator for the meetings is Joanne. She will be reaching out to you shortly following our implementation phase to schedule our first review meeting. At this meeting, we will incorporate the budgeting, the 401(k) plan, and the insurance discussion. (Joanne)

Our firm is looking forward to beginning this journey with you. Over time, I am confident that you will find a soul in your financial plan, but for now I look forward to getting started. I will call you next week to check in.

Best regards.

Cordially,

Larry Morgan, CFP®

cc: Paul Hushingbuck, Barbara Foster, and Joanne McGlaughlin

Linda placed the letter back into her pocketbook and Tom put the car on cruise control.

"Larry wanted us to get together with him, so I'll call him this week and get us a date," Linda said.

"Good idea. You know, I was thinking that when Larry comes to see us, it wouldn't be a bad idea for Greg to get together with him to discuss the money he made with the sale of his art. What do you think?" asked Tom.

"I think that's a good idea," she said. "I'll arrange that too."

As they sped along toward home, they were thinking about the financial planning road that lay ahead of them. It was fraught with possible traffic jams, speed traps, and potholes. But despite all of that, they could see their goals and were enjoying the feeling of moving toward them.

CHAPTER 17

Tom and Linda Begin Their Plan

"There should be a trumpet heralding the start of a new plan on the day New Account forms are signed," Larry said to Paul, who was looking at the piles of forms on the conference table with red "sign here" stickers peeking out from the sides.

"You seem to be in a good mood today," Paul noted.

"I am. Today is the day we launch, set sail, break ground—whatever analogy you like. I love to start the dig. You dig?" Larry smiled at his playful twist on words.

Paul began fastidiously flipping through the documents, making certain that no page or document was overlooked.

"Larry, as a reminder, please let them know that there will likely be more forms that need to be signed. I can tell that with this many accounts there will be some unknown form or requirement that will pop up after we submit."

"OK," Larry said.

Through a window, Larry saw Linda and Tom entering the office. It was 12:15 p.m. As Joanne set out a plate of deli sandwiches, Larry walked into the reception area to greet the Bells.

"Welcome, Tom. Hi, Linda," Larry said brightly.

In the conference room, Linda remarked how nice it had

been for Joanne to call her ahead of time and ask what they would like for lunch.

"Everything you guys do seems planned," she said.

"That's us, we love to plan ahead," Larry said with pride.

Linda and Tom made lunch plates for themselves, and Paul and Larry did the same. They ate first, before business, as Larry felt business should never be conducted on an empty stomach. Over lunch, the Bells talked about their trip to Longwood Gardens and the pride they felt in the economics associated with the day trip. Also, Linda updated everyone on her mother's progress. "Things are getting better, but it's slow going," Linda said.

Larry was aware that Tom had to return to work promptly by 1:30 p.m., so in the remaining thirty minutes, he asked Paul to lead them through the signing of the paperwork which would begin their planning relationship.

They signed as Paul pointed out and explained each form to them. He was quick to answer their questions about the forms so that there would be no confusion. He also provided them with a copy of mandatory disclosure documents that explained the rights and obligations of the custodian and record keeper of the accounts.

Paul mentioned that he would take a few minutes before they left to provide an overview of these documents.

"Do I need to read all of this?" Linda asked, glancing at the lengthy disclosure forms.

"What I would suggest," Larry said, "is that you take the documents home with you. It is up to you if you want to read them after our meeting, but it is my recommendation that you do so and to please call Paul or me if you have any questions.

They are fairly straightforward." He was well aware that getting the process started was overwhelming for many people, and was often interspersed with many questions and emotions.

By signing New Account forms, it meant Tom's and Linda's dreams were being put into motion; it was the first action step to seeing their dreams come true.

Their hearts were beating fast with the reality of the intangibilities and the uncertainty of the future as they began the long walk toward reaching their goals. As they signed their names at the bottom of countless documents, they could feel a palpable sense of control.

After she'd signed the final paper, Linda placed the pen on the table. Paul leaned back in his chair, holding all of the forms, and flipped through them page by page to make certain that no signature spots were missed. The room was silent as he worked. Finally, Paul looked up at Larry and nodded. "All looks good," he said.

"Well, Linda and Tom, today we begin," Larry said. "Welcome to the start of your financial plan. How do you feel?"

"Honey, please forgive me for jumping in," Tom said, holding Linda's arm, "but for the first time, I honestly feel good about our financial future. I feel as though all of my work and effort for so long, all of the money that I have made and hope to make will someday add up to something. My only regret is that we didn't do this sooner. But the way I see it, we retired in reverse. We traveled and saw the world, ate well, and did a lot of things that only retired people do. Right now, my focus is to save enough so I can slow down and be protected. That is my goal, or my dream, as you say, Larry. Quite frankly, it's all one and the same."

Linda was speechless. She was thrilled to hear her husband speak about savings in this way and the value he saw in planning. It reminded her of her youth, and the mother who'd taught her how to save.

"Linda, did you want to add anything?" asked Larry.

"The only thing that I would add, because my husband summed it up so well," she said with a smile, "is thank you. Thank you, Larry, and you too, Paul, and Joanne. And, please tell Barbara too. Thank you for all of your patience with us, for your help, and most of all, for believing in us. For believing we can reach our goals, all I can say is thank you."

Tom added that he wanted them to talk to Greg about some money he'd made selling artwork, to which Larry responded, "Absolutely."

Then Larry coached them through the call that he recommended they make to their current financial representative, Mr. Sullivan.

After Larry wrote himself a reminder to speak to Greg, he stood up and hugged Linda. Paul did the same. Both men shook hands with Tom. The start of their plan was underway.

Soon, Larry knew, the soul of their plan would emerge, the inner life of every financial plan.

PART THREE

Planning with Parents and Children

CHAPTER 18

Greg Bell

For Greg, the sale of the painting *Serving Coffee* was an affirmation of his career. With the sale, Greg was motivated to sell more artwork, which had been a goal since he was a child with dreams of working as a professional artist.

One of the challenging aspects in the fulfillment of this goal, however, was Greg's lack of knowledge in financial matters—a conundrum that became evident with the sale of that painting. At first, Greg wondered what he should do with the check that he received. Although his mother happily deposited it into his savings account at the bank, he wrestled with questions about what to actually do with the money. Should he buy more supplies to make more paintings, save it for the future, or save some and use some?

When his mother and father returned from their day trip to Longwood Gardens, he was happy that they suggested he call Joanne and make an appointment to meet with their new financial planner, Larry Morgan. He did so and booked an appointment for the very next day.

When Greg arrived at Larry's office for his appointment, Greg naturally took note of the paintings that adorned the walls.

Most depicted scenes of cities and parks. Apparently, Larry had a preference for landscape art, Greg noted. He also imagined one of his paintings displayed on a wall in an office like this. Greg sat down and within minutes heard a voice in the hallway, and a lanky man with a smiling face appeared.

"Hi, you must be Greg. It's nice to meet you again. I'm Larry."

"Cool, thanks," said Greg. They shook hands.

Greg and Larry walked together to the conference room.

"Your mother tells me you're studying to be a professional artist. How far along are you?" Larry said as he indicated where Greg should be seated. He wrote Greg's name on the top of a yellow pad. "Yes, um, I'm a sophomore," said Greg nervously.

Larry took great interest as Greg explained all about his program of study. Larry also wanted to know how Greg had become interested in painting, something that Greg was delighted to share. Greg found Larry to be a keen listener, as well as easy to talk to.

"I think the business aspect of being an artist is interesting," said Larry.

"Personally, I find it confusing. Y'know, my college offers a course called Financial Literacy, but it'll be two more years before I get to take it."

They began a conversation about the cost of making and selling paintings and focused in on the profit of the enterprise. Larry walked over to his dry-erase board so he could show Greg a visual representation of the analysis. "Are you familiar with the term profit margin?" Larry asked.

"Sort of. Is that like what you make on your sale, the profit?"

"Exactly," said Larry. "Let's try to figure out the profit margin of one of your pieces of art. What is the name of the one you just sold?"

"The painting was called *Serving Coffee*."

"Perfect," Larry said, as he picked up a blue marker and wrote the name of the artwork on the board. "How much did you sell it for?"

"I sold it for $1,875," Greg said, and Larry wrote the sales price on the board.

"Next, we need to identify the categories of what you spent in creating the artwork," said Larry, still writing.

Greg rattled off the different supplies he had used. "I bought the canvas, I actually made the frame myself but needed to buy the wood. Then there was the paint, the turpentine, and the brushes."

Larry turned to Greg and asked, "Anything else?"

"Yes, my parents did spend some money for me to meet with my art teacher, who guided me along as I worked."

"OK," Larry said as he wrote down the category for this expense. "And were there any other costs?"

"I think that's it," said Greg, scratching his chin in thought.

"Now I would like to know the cost of each of these items," Larry said.

Greg provided his best estimates for each category and Larry entered each cost next to the appropriate category. Finally, Larry asked Greg about how much income tax he thought he might owe on the income.

Greg said, "I have no clue."

"No problem," Larry said. "Let's use 15 percent just for this example."

Larry took out a calculator and punched in a few numbers and wrote on the board the following:

Serving Coffee Profit Calculation	
Painting Sales Price:	$1,875
Less Cost of Goods Sold:	
Canvas	($60)
Paint—Estimated	($105)
Self-Made Frame	($25)
Specialist's Consulting Fee	($125)
Subtotal Cost of Goods Sold	($315)
Net Profit Before Tax	$1,560
Less: Income Taxes (15%)	($234)
Net Profit After Tax	**$1,326**

Larry put down his markers, and sat back down.

Greg had a surprised look on his face.

"For the painting that you sold," Larry said, and picked up the calculator again and entered some figures, "I estimate that your profit margin was 71 percent."

"Very interesting," Greg replied.

"How many hours did it take you to make the painting?" asked Larry.

Greg thought for a minute, and said that it took him about thirty-five hours, over a period of about three weeks.

Larry took out his calculator again, stood up, and wrote on the board: $38/hour.

He double underlined it. "This is what your time was worth," he announced, and then put his markers away and sat back down.

"Wow, that seems really good," Greg said in astonishment.

"I agree, not bad at all," Larry said, and smiled.

Greg shared that he did not know what to do with the money that was now in his savings account. Larry explained that there was a process in financial planning for making decisions about what to do with money earned. He stressed that decisions should always be made in the context of an overall plan. Larry spent the next several minutes putting together a simple financial plan for Greg. The check was an asset, as were the other pieces of art that Greg could make and sell.

Greg's net worth statement looked like this on the conference room screen:

Assets:		Liabilities:	
Cash	$1,875	School Loan	$18,700
Art Inventory	$30,000	Credit Card Debt	$2,500
Total	$31,875	Total	$21,200

Total Net Worth: **$10,675**

Then, Larry and Greg put together an estimate of what his school loan would look like after college, which his parents said they would likely help him pay, and also his expectations of net income.

Larry portrayed an estimate of the amount of net income Greg could make as an artist, using a calculation of the time it took him to finish a painting, along with the expected sales on a monthly basis. Being conservative, the cash flow report looked like this:

Cash Flow Report	
Art Income	$25,000
Less: Business Expenses	($11,475)
Net Business Income	$13,525
Less: Living Expenses	($7,000)
Less: Income Taxes	($1,500)
Surplus/Deficit	**$5,025**

Larry then applied a rate of inflation and a hypothetical expectation of business growth. In the end, if everything worked according to the estimates and if his artwork continued to sell, then he concluded that Greg should have additional surplus income in the future.

"Based on this analysis, you should be faced with the same dilemma each year, which is what to do with surpluses," concluded Larry.

Greg was fascinated, and feeling very motivated about his future. "If I make enough money, I could possibly move out of my parents' house and live on my own. That's one of my goals."

"My recommendation in the beginning while you are getting started," said Larry, "is to reinvest half of your surplus back into the business for new paint supplies, canvases, and studio expenses, and to invest the other half in a long-term investment account."

"I think that's good, but why fifty-fifty?" Greg asked.

"Because there's no way to come up with an exact percentage. So when in doubt, I always like to go with a fifty-fifty approach. It's the best way to hedge a decision."

"Cool," said Greg.

"So today," Larry said, "you should plan on doing just that, keep half for your business and let's get the other half invested."

"Sounds good," Greg said, "but invested in what?" He looked confused.

"What do you know about investments, say stocks or bonds?" asked Larry.

"Well, my grandfather bought some shares of Disney stock for me when I was first born. I actually have a colorful certificate with all of the Disney characters on it still hanging on a wall in my bedroom."

Larry smiled. "Do you follow the price of that stock?" he asked.

"Actually no, I just know that I have some of it. I think 50 shares," Greg said.

"OK, and what about bonds? Do you have any savings bonds from when you were born?"

"I think so, but I'm not sure," Greg laughed, "I feel like I should know more than I know."

Larry explained that most people didn't really understand what it meant to own a stock or a bond. He explained to Greg the reasons why public companies issue stocks, which was typically that they had a need for raising capital to run their operations or to expand, and that they went to the public to look for funds in exchange for ownership shares in the business.

Larry asked Greg to think of himself as Walt Disney, the

artist, who was making sketches of a little mouse. Walt had a vision of making movies around characters that he was drawing, so he needed funds to make the movies.

"Walt gave people two options for investing—one was to become a part owner, which meant that if the movie did well, there would be the potential to make a lot of money; but if the movie bombed, they could also lose it all."

"OK," Greg said. He was listening intently.

"Another option for Walt was borrowing," Larry said. "The public could lend Walt the money, and he would pay interest on the loan and then pay back the initial amount." Larry explained that *ownership* was stock investing and *lending* was bond investing.

"That's really cool, I never knew that," Greg said, "So, the shares I have on my wall mean that I am a part owner of Disney, the theme park and all?"

"Yes, that is how the system works, and those United States savings bonds you have means that you are also a lender to the US government; and for doing that, the government pays you interest. One day down the road when you ask the government for your borrowed funds back, they'll give you what you gave them initially, plus interest for the loan."

"I like it," said Greg, "I'll have to ask my mother about them. I'm not sure where they are."

Then Greg asked about investing his recent deposit.

Larry had a recommendation—to invest in various sectors of stocks and bonds and spread the risk. The reason he liked it for Greg, he said, was that it provided diversification and asset allocation. Greg asked Larry to explain these concepts.

"Well, let's think about the artwork you create. Do all of your paintings always have a buyer?"

"I wish," Greg said.

"So, there's a risk when you put up a few paintings for sale that some will actually sell and others will not."

Greg nodded.

"That's diversification, spreading the risk around," said Larry. "So instead of investing in just Disney stock, it is historically beneficial to own several different stocks, some of which will go up in value and others that will likely go down."

Larry explained that with a concept like diversification as a strategy, it would not protect against loss or guarantee a profit. Rather, it was used to help guide an overall plan to help manage the ups and downs in the market.

"But that's only half of the story. In the marketplace, just as there were millions of people who wanted to be stock owners, there were also many who saw value in being lenders, and not owners. There were also different kinds of companies, countries, and government municipalities that looked for people who would loan them money, and to whom they would then pay it back with interest."

"So, do I need to be both an owner and a lender? Why's that?" asked Greg.

"Excellent question," Larry said. "So there is a mysterious thing that happens when millions of people invest in stocks and bonds at the same time. We notice that often when bonds are in favor, stocks are out of favor, and vice versa."

"Oh, you mean it can vary at different times of the year?" asked Greg.

"Yes," Larry said, "but it could be different days. That's why I recommend different types of investments. I think it's good to be a lender on some days and an owner on others. The formal term for owning different types or classes of investments is asset allocation. Though asset allocation is a strategy we use, it does not ensure a profit or protect against a loss. It's similar to painting sales. I'm sure there are times when certain paintings sell and other times when they do not."

Greg sat straighter in his chair. "Actually, it's interesting that you say that because I heard in class the other day that oil paintings sell more in the winter time and watercolors in the summer."

"Perfect," Larry replied. "So think of the oils like owning stocks, and the watercolors like the bonds. Similar to paintings, sometimes stocks are better investments, and at other times, bonds perform better."

"So, do you tell me when I should buy stocks versus bonds?"

"Actually, Greg, no one can ever tell you that. We call that timing the market, and no one knows that information, since the markets are unpredictable. Financial advisors like me are students of a different school of thought, which says we never try to time things, but rather stay invested in both stocks and bonds at all times. So, typically, if you want more risk, you own a greater percentage of stocks, and for less risk, you own a greater percentage of bonds."

Larry explained that the key was to adjust the ratios of each, depending upon one's tolerance for volatility and one's time horizon. Larry took Greg through the same questionnaire that he'd completed with Linda and Tom, and it indicated that Greg was a balanced investor. Larry explained that this meant that 60 percent of the investments would be in the stock market at all times, and 40 percent would be in the bond market. "The most interesting thing about all of this, Greg, is that you have taught me something today about oil painting sales versus watercolor sales, which is that they are not correlated. This is a great way to understand stocks and bonds. Thank you for this."

"No problem. I'm glad I could teach you something new," Greg said.

Larry grinned and asked Greg if he could see his work sometime, to which Greg replied that it was all on display on his website, but that he could show him some canvases the next time he visited his parents.

Larry called Joanne and asked her to prepare New Account forms. Greg signed some forms, and left Larry's office feeling energized and confident with his newfound understanding of investing. When he went home, he headed into his basement studio and began a new painting. About an hour into Greg's new painting, he heard a loud shriek from upstairs. He dropped his brushes, and in the process accidentally smeared the new artwork with his elbow. He ran into the kitchen and found his mother on the phone. "Mom, what happened? Is everything all right?" Greg huffed in panic.

His mother was standing by the kitchen table laughing as she held the phone.

"Jessica and Nicole are having another baby!" she said. "Baby number four!"

CHAPTER 19

Jessica and Nicole

On a Sunday morning several weeks since her daughter's big announcement, Linda decided to stop by Jessica and Nicole's home, just for a minute. She wanted to drop off some items on her way to the hospital, where she was planning to discharge her mother and take her home. Linda liked to help Jess and Nicki with small errands, as it gave her a chance to stop by and see the grandchildren.

Helen had reached a point where her strength was improving. She was to continue care in her home, along with undergoing physical and occupational therapy. Linda was looking forward to getting her mother out of the hospital, but from the minute she opened Jessica's front door, she knew that she was likely going to be late getting there.

"Hello?" Linda said timidly, pushing the door open, and raising her voice. The sound of scampering feet could be heard from within the house, and then little voices shouting, "Grandmom! Grandmom's here!"

Lila, the oldest, was the first one to greet her in the foyer. She wrapped her little arms tightly around Linda's legs. Then her younger brother, Jimmy, came toddling right behind her with a pacifier in his mouth. When he saw Linda, he jumped up and down, clapping. "Where's Oliver?" Linda asked Lila.

"Watching TV. I'll take you." Lila took Linda's hand and led her into the family room. As she walked through the house, she noticed it was especially disorganized. Toys were everywhere, a filled laundry basket was sitting on the dining room table, and as she made her way past the kitchen, she could see a pile of dirty dishes in the sink.

"Where's Mommy?" Linda asked Lila.

"I think she is in the bathroom." In a loud voice she screamed, "Mommy!" and ran up the staircase.

Just then, Jessica appeared.

"Hi, Mom," she casually said as she kissed her mother on the cheek.

"Jess, can I help you at all? Let me vacuum, please."

"Mom, it's fine, we'll get to it, I promise. Here, let me grab these." Jessica took the two plastic bags her mother was carrying.

Ever since Jimmy, their third child, was born, Jessica and Nicole had been challenged by the sheer amount of work it took to run their home and raise the children. Plus, with Nicole now pregnant again, it seemed there was more housework that needed to be done. The two of them were exhausted. Also, Nicole was having a difficult pregnancy. With an unusual amount of morning sickness, her doctor advised taking it easy. Between managing the house, a work schedule, and the kids, the couple felt as though life had opened up and swallowed them alive.

Nicole came into the kitchen barefoot, kissed Linda hello, and thanked her for the help.

"Here, I got this special for you," Linda said as she handed her a large cylinder that held a poster.

"What is it?" Nicole said as she lifted open the cap of the tube.

"It's a stenciled saying from someone named Earl Nightingale. Apparently, he was a famous motivational speaker years ago. Anyway, I saw it at the card store and thought you could stencil it up on one of the kid's walls."

Nicole pulled it out and read the quote out loud: "Never give up on a dream just because of the time it will take to accomplish it. The time will pass anyway."

"Well, what do you think?" Linda asked.

"It's a little sad," Nicole said, and she began to cry.

"Oh, honey, I'm sorry," Linda said, as she grabbed a napkin off the kitchen table and handed it to her.

"No, it's very nice and thoughtful of you. I just have been so emotional lately," she said as she wiped her tears.

"It's OK," Linda said. "It's probably your hormones."

Jessica jumped in and said, "Well, I can tell you I like the quote, but the part about time passing anyway, I can see why Nicki thinks it's a bit sad."

Linda sighed. "I guess I've been channeling the brevity-of-life thing lately with all of my visits to the hospital."

"Wait, didn't Grandma always have that other saying of hers . . . let me see . . . oh yes. 'Time goes by like a dream in the night,'" Jessica recited, with a wave of her hands.

"Yes, that was it!" Linda said smiling.

"By the way, aren't you supposed to get her out of the hospital today?" Jessica asked.

Linda nodded. "I'm meeting with the social worker in about

half an hour. In fact, I should get going." She looked at her watch. As Jessica and Nicole walked her to the door, Linda said, "I was just telling Larry last week that no matter how bad she gets, I would never have her go to a nursing home—"

"Wait a second, who's Larry?" Jessica interrupted.

"Larry Morgan. He's our financial planner. You met him in the hospital, remember on that first day?"

"Oh, yeah," Jessica said. "I didn't realize who that guy was. Wait a minute, he's your financial planner?"

"Yes, your father and I hired him and his firm to help us with our financial planning."

Linda went on to explain why they'd decided to get help. She also casually mentioned to Jessica and Nicole that they might want to meet with Larry someday.

Jessica said, "You're kidding, right?"

"I did say 'someday,'" stammered Linda.

Jessica proceeded to go on a rant about how she and Nicole were just too busy right now to make time for anything. They hadn't been sleeping well, Nicole had no energy, the house was impossible to stay on top of, and there were ten other reasons they had no time. Jessica went on and on.

"But on a positive note," she said, "Clarke and I were thinking about moving to a bigger office. The practice is growing to the point where we need more space, and we may need to hire or look for a third dentist." Clarke Addison was Jessica's partner in their dental practice.

Just then, the kitchen door swung open with a loud bang. Nicole yelled, "Aaahhh!" in surprise, and Linda put her hand to her chest. All three kids came into the kitchen wailing, with

Jimmy accusing Oliver of taking his train and Oliver pointing at Lila, who he claimed knocked over his Legos and then hit him.

Linda took this as a sign that she should be going. Jessica took the children and Nicole walked Linda to the door. Nicole then quietly thanked her. "Thank you for the neat stencil. You know, you're right, it would be a good idea to one day meet with your financial planner," she said. "I think about it all of the time. Jess is just too stressed right now. She and Clarke are making big decisions, and they really need help."

"I know. I worry about you two. I also wished Tom and I had done it sooner. It's harder the later you get to it."

"Well, let your guy, Larry, know that one day I will call," said Nicole.

"Will do. I'll text you his contact information. His scheduler is Joanne."

It took another ten minutes for Linda to leave, as each of the three grandchildren had just one last thing to show her. She'd discovered that one of the surprising joys of grandchildren was the playing without the parenting.

CHAPTER 20

Helen Leaves the Hospital

The social worker at the hospital told Linda that according to her mother's chart, the doctors felt that her condition might improve over time. To Linda, however, her previously vibrant mother now had the appearance of a sickly ninety-year-old. She was hunched over in the seat of her wheelchair, and her hair had lost the rich, silver luster it had before she was admitted eight weeks ago.

Hospital standards required a social worker's review of the physician's care plan with all patients and family members prior to leaving. The plan had been put together by a multi-disciplinary team at Vineland Main. In a small beige office, Linda and Helen spoke to Rachel, a professional and friendly social worker.

After the meeting with Larry several weeks before to prepare for this day, Linda had researched several home care agencies in Vineland. She had met with a few of the agency managers and asked friends who'd been in similar situations about what agencies they'd used. She settled on an agency in Vineland called Premier Home Care. Just a few days before, when Linda knew that her mother would be leaving, Premier arranged for Linda and Helen to meet several potential home health aides. Each aide had a different skill set and personality.

Linda really liked an affable home health aide named Betty Ann. She was a large, capable woman from Jamaica with strong, calloused hands, which gripped hers firmly when they first said hello. Linda could feel a positive energy from Betty Ann that she liked, and that she thought would be good for her mother. In Jamaica, Betty Ann, the mother of four children, had actually been a full-time nurse in a hospital. She had come to America for a better life.

"You and my mom have that in common," Linda said when they first started talking. "My mother came to America for the same thing as you, to search for a better life."

Betty Ann reached over and rubbed Helen's back, and said, "Is that right, Mrs. D? I know you and I are going to get along just fine." And she let out a hearty laugh.

Linda carefully evaluated how each care provider interviewing for the position interacted with her mother. Linda took the "care" part of the profession's title very seriously. While Rachel reviewed the medications list and discussed the need for grab bars in the bathroom, Betty Ann arrived and peeked her head in the office. "Good morning, Mom, and Miss Linda," Betty Ann said. She spoke with a booming British Caribbean accent and was carrying her suitcase.

Linda and Helen were happy to see her. Linda asked Betty Ann politely if she would be kind enough to wait as they finished up with Rachel. From her wheelchair, Helen waved feebly. The stroke had partially paralyzed Helen's vocal cords. Happy to have finally exchanged her hospital gown for everyday clothing, she appeared very glad to be leaving, as she sat patiently next to Linda with her hands folded.

The social worker went over Helen's care plan. She explained to Linda that the cost of live-in care with Premier was $187 per day and that Medicare would likely pay for some of it during the first one hundred days. Specifically, she explained, only the care associated with wound care for the bedsore on Helen's lower back would be covered. Rachel told her that Premier would be sending out a registered nurse to perform this service.

Linda nodded. The social worker also warned Linda that the costs associated with Betty Ann would not be covered under Medicare, as that does not cover custodial care activities associated with basic activities of daily living such as eating, dressing, bathing, toileting, and transferring. "Those services are full private pay, understood?"

"Yes, understood," Linda said calmly.

"So you understand then that all of the care that she receives in her home will be paid for from your mother's assets and income," the social worker said perfunctorily.

"Yes."

Paying for services worried Linda. Though she had met with Larry several weeks before and Larry felt comfortable with her mother's resources, she decided to call him again from the hospital after they finished the meeting.

It was Sunday, so she thought that she would just leave him a message; however, much to her surprise, Larry answered the phone.

"So sorry to bother you on a weekend," Linda said. "I was going to leave you a message, but—"

"This is fine, Linda. Is everything OK?" Larry said in a concerned tone.

Linda explained what was happening with her mother and the costs involved. Larry listened carefully and assured her that all would be fine. Since he had all of Helen's resources placed into her financial plan from a few weeks ago, he offered to plug in the actual expenses and run a report that would predict how long her resources would last using the actual costs of care. "Linda, I will call you tomorrow and we'll go over everything. My hunch is that all will work out well."

"That would be great," Linda said. "Oh, by the way, before I forget, my daughter-in-law, Nicole Thompson, you know, Jessica's wife, will be calling to get on your calendar soon. Something has come up at Jess's business and your help is needed. I told her to call Joanne directly. Is that OK?"

"Of course," said Larry. "I look forward to meeting the last members of the Bell clan."

Linda was very appreciative that Larry had made himself so available to help with the myriad of planning issues that had arisen with the family.

"By the way, I'm happy your mother is finally going home," Larry said.

"Thank you," Linda replied. "So are we." As her mother could not write, Linda signed the discharge papers, and the three of them—Helen, Betty Ann, and Linda—left the hospital together.

CHAPTER 21

Reviewing Helen's Plan

Larry's mind was abuzz as he drove over to meet Linda at Helen's house. Financial planning began with mundane data like account statements, copies of wills, insurance policies, and monthly expenses, and then over time, the intangible pieces like life circumstances, health histories, dreams, goals, and desires came into the plan. The data combined with the circumstances formed a plan's structure. The planner edified a plan with exceptional listening skills, a good value system, wisdom, logic, ethics, and a strong knowledge of taxes, investments, and insurance.

When it all came together over time, a plan came alive. Larry could feel it.

He was reminded once again of his belief that a financial plan was not just about taking the facts and using them to generate reports, but rather that a plan had a life force to it, one that existed between planner and client. This was the *anima bekker*—the soul of the plan. It existed when a commitment was made by people who cared about pursuing goals together.

Early in his career, Larry had some clients that were focused solely on investing, with planning as a secondary consideration.

Managing assets without the context of a plan created a different kind of relationship. It typically existed around the performance of the account; and often when the stock market fell, so would the spirit of the relationship.

But the bedrock of successful financial planning could be distilled down to one important point, alone and universal for all time and for all planners: In order for a financial plan to succeed fully, the planner had to genuinely care.

It was simple care that bound people together in the success of their plan. Where there was care, there was hope, and with hope came the possibility of accomplishing dreams.

"I don't know what we are going to do," Linda said as she paced around her mother's kitchen.

She handed Larry a glass of water, and she noted his calm demeanor as he thanked her.

Seated at the kitchen table, Larry was taking notes. His first interest was hearing about the progress Linda's mother had made over the last several weeks. Larry followed Principle 6 of the CFP Board Code of Ethics, Professionalism, when he acted in a manner that demonstrated "exemplary professional conduct."

"I'm going to talk softly, since my mother is in the other room," Linda said, and in a quiet voice, she explained that Helen had at first been unable to get out of bed, but now with assistance could get up from a chair and stand for a minute or so. "The entire left side of her body was paralyzed," Linda said. "The doctor said that she needs full-time care, and that at her age it's unclear whether she will ever get her functionality back."

"How has she handled her situation?" asked Larry.

"Not well," answered Linda. "She has been very depressed

about it. The other day she kept saying to me that she would be dead soon and that this life was not a life at all." Linda began to cry. Larry offered Linda a napkin from a holder on the table.

"Thank you," Linda said and she took it and wiped her eyes.

When she'd regained her composure, Larry shifted into business mode. He and Linda sat down at the kitchen table and, with the help of his laptop, went through Helen's resources again. Larry noticed that there were numerous bills Linda had recently begun helping her mother pay. Linda had brought out the home care agency agreement for Larry to see, along with the bills, some of which had been presented to Medicare for reimbursement. Larry reinforced the fact that her mother had a fairly strong cushion of savings, mostly CDs and municipal bonds. "I like that Betty Ann is there for her. I could not do it alone. She's just terrific," Linda said.

Larry nodded as he added numbers from the papers to a spreadsheet on his laptop. After several minutes, he looked up at Linda again. "OK, I think I'm good. This is very high-level, but based on the cost of full-time care from Betty Ann, plus inflation, along with Helen's available resources—and applying a very conservative rate of return for growth—I estimate that she has at least sixteen years of spending before she would exhaust her assets."

"Really?" said Linda. Larry reiterated that this was using the most conservative approach. He explained that if he modified the assumptions to assume more expenses in the future, then the run-down time would be shorter, and if more return came from the investments, the outcome would be improved.

Linda had been uncertain of how long her mother's resources

would last, and felt much better with this information. Larry explained that doing this work and tracking the progress was the gateway to a financial plan for Helen. This was also, he said, a good example of how decisions concerning someone's welfare could actually be solved through a process of getting things organized so resources could be projected forward.

"Linda, you don't have to worry. Everything will be all right," Larry said with confidence.

"So, what do we do now that we know this? What's next?" Linda said with an air of relief.

"Well, your mother does need some simple monitoring of expenses in relationship to her assets. This must be done with regularity. If you want, we can incorporate this into your planning processes. It would not be difficult to do it. If you bring the information, we will monitor it every ninety days, just like we are going to do with your financial plan."

"Will this be expensive?"

"Not at all. I'm expecting that we can do it as a part of our engagement with you, so without adding additional cost. That is the goal, at least from what I see this year. Next year, I noticed that some of her CDs and bonds mature, so we might need to get a little involved in her wealth management. But the way I see it, we will need cash to pay for her expenses, so right now I'm only thinking about having cash on hand." Larry closed his laptop.

"Makes sense," Linda said.

Linda told Larry how grateful she was for his input, and they went into the living room to sit with Helen. The television was on. Betty Ann excused herself to go to the bathroom. "Mom,

Larry and I went through all of your finances, and you'll be fine. You don't have to worry about a thing. Sound good?"

Helen was slumped in a chair, with her head tilted to the left. With a show of great effort, she mustered a smile.

CHAPTER 22

In the Backyard

One week later, Greg stood in the backyard of his home trying to focus on a new painting. His subject was the small creek that ran through the swath of woods adjacent to the house's east side. It was a sunny day, and his paint set glistened colorfully in the brilliant light.

Greg stared intently at his subject, then dabbed a few colors on the canvas, and used his sleeve to smear the paint. He dabbed again, then stood back and squinted. He was having a hard time concentrating. He moved the brush forward, but then lost focus again. Finally, he dropped his head in defeat. The investments he'd made with Larry were the cause of his unease.

Earlier in the day, during breakfast, he'd read a newspaper article about a possible recession looming, and it didn't sound good. Also, the day before, he'd heard on the news that the stock market had just dropped in a big way. So as he attempted to paint, Greg found himself with worried thoughts about losing the money he'd made from his sale. Greg took off his painter's smock and set down his brushes. He decided to call Larry's office and see if he could stop by to have Larry or Paul go through his investment account with him. Joanne told him to come right over.

When Greg arrived at the office, Joanne was standing on a chair by her desk near the waiting area. She was reaching upward, trying to unscrew an overhead lightbulb.

"Do you need some help?" Greg said.

"Thanks for asking," Joanne said, "but I'm just about done," and then she stepped down from the chair. She patted her hair back into place and resumed a professional demeanor as she sat down behind her desk. "You are going to meet with Paul, as Larry isn't in. Is that OK?" She referred to the schedule on her computer, which also indicated that Jessica and Nicole were going to come in later in the week.

"That's fine," Greg said. "I only had a quick question about something in my account. Thank you so much."

Joanne directed Greg into the conference room, and Paul entered a moment later.

A financial planner has to be ready for the unexpected. A planning practice is like a large industrial machine with hundreds of parts moving at the same time. At a moment's notice, one or two gears could stop moving, break, or change direction.

Once seated, Paul picked up a pen and asked Greg, "So, what's on your mind?" Greg explained that he was worried about losing everything he had invested. He'd been listening to the news and it all seemed bad. Also, it was reported the day before that the Dow Jones Industrial Average dropped one hundred points.

Paul explained to Greg that the Dow Jones Industrial Average is comprised of thirty stocks that are the leaders in their industries and are widely held by investors. "Let me ask you this," Paul asked slowly. "What do you think might happen?"

"I'm afraid I will lose all of the money I made from my painting," Greg said.

Paul was attempting to get to the source of Greg's worry. Typically, he knew, behind every concern like this one was a bigger concern around something related to planning.

"And then what?" Paul asked. He was challenging Greg so he could follow his thinking, and he discovered that Greg had a bigger goal in mind: He wanted to use the money he'd invested to buy his own art studio someday. He was hoping to do this about ten years after college, or in approximately twelve years. Paul was connecting the fear to the plan.

Paul reviewed Greg's investment allocation to discern his risk. Greg's portfolio was 60 percent in stock-based investing and 40 percent in bonds and fixed income. Paul also reviewed Greg's Risk Tolerance Questionnaire, specifically his response to Question #5, about how he'd react if his investments suddenly declined by 15 percent. "You had said that you would not likely react and would stay the course. Is that still the case?" Paul asked.

Greg explained that it would be, as he really didn't need to use the assets at this time. Paul went over the portfolio, and explained that the portfolio was not just invested in the few stocks of the Dow Jones, but in thousands of other investments. He pointed out that even though large cap stocks had fallen, nearly 50 percent of Greg's account had gone up, as bonds, small cap stocks, and real estate had done well.

Paul's words made Greg remember the principles of asset

allocation, in terms of the analogy of watercolors and oil paintings that Larry had used to explain the concept. As he did this,
he took a deep breath and told Paul that he still felt comfortable
with the initial recommendation of 60 percent in equities and
40 percent in fixed income.

Paul assured Greg that the worry he was feeling was well
founded.

But overall, Greg felt relieved. Paul's explanation on the
principles of diversification had been very helpful.

Greg left the office feeling appreciative of having guides to
the very confusing world of investments. But above all else, Greg
felt good that somebody took the time to listen to him and his
financial worries.

In financial planning, a planner must practice the art of listening. When waves roll into shore, they generally roll steady
and even; but every once in a while, one lands just a bit louder
than the rest.

It is this wave that the planner must hear.

CHAPTER 23

Pre-Meeting Preparation for Jessica and Nicole

When Larry came into the office, he was unaware that Greg had just left.

"You missed young Mr. Bell," Joanne said as Larry took off his suit jacket. She explained that Greg had been worried about his account, but Paul handled it.

"That's great," he said. "Our teamwork is really essential. Can you please ask Paul to meet me in the conference room?"

When Paul entered, Larry was seated at the table, writing on a notepad. He explained he was working on the agenda for the meeting with Jessica and Nicole.

"Well, I spoke to Nicole today and her main concerns were the new baby, the possibility of Jessica passing away, college planning for the kids, not having any savings, and in the far distance, retirement."

Paul and Larry discussed that an additional issue to explore was whether there was a buy-sell agreement at the business that would cover a sickness or death contingency between Jessica and her partner. "Actually, Linda told me things were in transition in the business." They wrote down a few questions on the notepad:

1. How did Jessica's business pay her?

2. Did Jessica or Nicole have debts from college, or the business, or on credit cards?

3. If Jessica's partner, Dr. Addison, were to become disabled, how would Jessica cover all of the patients?

4. How healthy were Jessica and Nicole?

Paul said, "Baby four, Larry, it's like you always say . . ."

"What's that?"

"Four's the charm," said Paul, laughing.

"I never say that," said Larry with a smile. And then, his face grew serious. "You know, Paul, one of the things I so like about financial planning is the juxtaposition of facts and circumstances."

"Wait, Larry, I have to get out a dictionary. What was that word?"

Larry smiled. "You know, juxtaposition—the way one element contrasts with another. Sometimes the facts of a financial plan unfold this way, like planning for both life and death, or savings and spending. All of it gets juxtaposed together in the same plan."

"Yes, I see," Paul said.

"What's weird," Larry went on, "is that I have noticed as I get older, these elements seem to unfold in an order."

"Really?" Paul said.

"Sure. Scientists are finding an order in everything from the stars in the galaxies to the atoms in our bodies, and I feel the same is true of a financial plan. There is an order to the way it comes to life. It's an organism, part of a much larger whole—bigger than it appears to be."

"You know, Larry, that's deep," Paul said. Then he paused thoughtfully and grinned. He raised his hand in the air and high-fived with Larry. "I really like that! But speaking of ordering, let's order in some lunch. I'm starving."

Larry laughed.

The two then spent the rest of the hour discussing the important points they wanted to address in their meeting with Jessica and Nicole at the end of the week. When they finished, Paul left Larry alone in the conference room.

He sat quietly with his eyes closed, meditating on his life and the closeness he felt with others' lives. He felt he had a mission to fulfill, one that emerged from deep within his heart—it was to help others prepare for the future so they were ready and confident for whatever lay ahead.

As he sat there, he felt suddenly overcome with gratitude for his ability to help others. He wondered, perhaps, if his work was part of some bigger plan. Financial planning was about reflection—quiet, thoughtful, unspoken reflection.

CHAPTER 24

Early Morning Conversation

Larry showed up at the office early on the day he was scheduled to meet with Nicole and Jessica. Barbara Foster came in about a half hour later.

"So, are you ready?" Barbara asked.

"If you're asking if I am ready to begin another financial plan, then yes, I'm up for the journey," Larry replied. "Paul and I met earlier this week and we have a full agenda of questions." Barbara's role as portfolio analyst meant that she developed portfolios based upon the present state of the economy, implemented cash deposits, and reviewed and watched the investment accounts. Her passion was fulfilled when she developed an investment portfolio that performed well, but with lower risk. She called this risk-adjusted return.

"Is that it, it's another journey?" Barbara chuckled.

"What else is it? You know better than anyone else that once I commit to a plan, I am in it with both feet," Larry said, and laughed.

"Do you think Nicole and Jessica will commit?"

"We'll see. They should be here in about thirty minutes. I know they have quite a few fears, but as usual, I prefer to learn about their dreams and goals first and then work from there. I think they have a lot to tell me."

Barbara nodded in agreement. "You know, Barbara, I look at it like this—when your dreams are kept bottled up and lay deep inside, untouched, I believe they're never born . . . they actually die in utero."

"I see," Barbara said and sipped her coffee.

"For me," Larry said, "that is the saddest death . . . the death of an unborn dream."

Barbara smiled and said, "You know, Larry, you're a real poet. You should write some of this stuff down one day. It would make an interesting book."

When Barbara left, Larry grabbed a pencil and a piece of paper. He wrote a note to himself, and then said under his breath, "You know something, I just might do that."

He placed the folded note in his pocket and left to finish getting ready for the visit from Jessica and Nicole. On the note was Larry's goal—to write a book about financial planning.

CHAPTER 25

Nicole and Jessica's Meeting

"How is your grandmother doing?" Larry said to Jessica as he wrote *Nicole Thompson and Jessica Bell—Financial Planning Meeting* at the top of a yellow notepad, along with the date.

Jessica looked tired, as though she hadn't slept in a few days.

"I would say she's doing fair. What do you think?" Jessica said and looked at Nicole.

Nicole was pulling her long brown hair into a ponytail. "I think Mom has her hands full. I mean, she is unbelievably there for Helen, like every day, but this whole thing has been upsetting for her."

"I know it's been hard," said Larry with a nod. Sometimes easing into a planning discussion reminded Larry of backing into a parking space in reverse—it required patience and sensitivity, and many small, slow movements. Larry shifted the conversation back to them.

"So," Larry said, "we are here to talk about your planning. I really appreciate your coming in today."

"I know you wanted to meet at the house," Nicole said, "but with the kids there, it's really tough to discuss anything."

Jessica nodded in agreement.

Larry said, "No problem. OK, let's start with a download."

"What's that?" Nicole asked.

"Tell me everything that you are worried about with your finances. No filter. Don't worry about how you order or say it. I'll sit back and take notes while you talk."

Nicole looked over at Jessica who was fiddling with a paperclip, and began. "I guess the first thing we're worried about is with the situation at the office. It's getting busier and Jess and Clarke are in need of a third partner."

"OK."

"As for me, you know I'm pregnant with our fourth child. So with Jess working, I'm worried about something happening to her, or vice versa. If something happens to me, how will she manage her job and the kids? Speaking of kids, I am worried about college. Some of our friends have started college savings accounts, and I'm worried that we haven't done anything like that yet, plus we don't have wills, and forget retirement." Nicole looked at Jessica, and said, "Jess, what do you think? Did I miss anything?"

Larry put down his pen and stretched his hands. "So Jessica, did you want to add anything?" he said.

"I only have one thing to add that worries me," Jessica said.

"What's that?"

"I need," she paused and looked at Nicole, "I mean, we need, a way to keep everything organized. Nicki and I get overwhelmed by the amount of time it takes to get stuff organized. I cannot conceive of making time to get any of this done. Just getting here today was, like, impossible."

Larry explained his role and how the process of financial

planning required the organization of projects, prioritization, and realistic strategies with time frames around their implementation. Then, there would be monitoring of everything. Larry told them that he and his entire team worked together. Paul and Joanne worked to keep things organized, Barbara watched over the investments, and Larry looked regularly at the big picture. He concluded by saying, "And having a financial planner can reduce the burden of needing to do everything on your own."

Jessica shared that her biggest challenge was time. She worried mostly about the practice and how to manage the growth.

"Speaking about the practice, the one thing I am interested to read is this copy of the shareholder's agreement that you and Clarke signed when you began it."

"Oh?" Jessica said as Larry held up the document she'd brought to the meeting in a folder with other documents.

"This document should specify what happens to either your or Clarke's interest in the company should either of you become permanently disabled, or if you should pass away."

"Really? I don't remember us even discussing it," Jessica said as she nervously linked and unlinked a pair of paper clips. Larry was not surprised to hear a business owner claim bewilderment about her own company's formation documents. When business owners joined together to form a business, there were generally only thoughts of good things happening, things like how the business would grow, profits would generate, and all would be good. Rarely did partners in a new business venture discuss the things that could go wrong.

Larry explained that the very best approach was to have a separate agreement, called a buy-sell agreement. "A buy-sell agreement is basically a business failure plan, akin to a pre-nuptial agreement in marriage. It specifies what would happen in the event of a disability, death, or other contingency. I usually recommend insurance coverage to fund it, should an unexpected catastrophe arise. The ultimate goal is the protection of the business," Larry said. "Without having looked over everything yet, does the term 'buy-sell agreement' sound familiar?"

"Not at all," said Jessica.

"So, next time we get together, I will spend more time on this topic," Larry said. "Given all that you shared today, we may want to have a separate meeting with Clarke and you, Jessica, just on this topic. Let's address this after we have completed your financial plan."

"OK," said Jessica. Larry knew it was easy to get overwhelmed, so therefore, pacing the process was essential. He completed a basic fact finder with Nicole and Jessica that gathered all of the key information such as dates of birth, addresses, the spelling of children's names, and other information that would be securely entered into the computer. He also covered the total process of financial planning with them, which included the firm's approach to investing, preparation for contingencies with insurance, and fees.

"I know this is probably a ridiculous question," asked Nicole, "but all the information we gave you like our statements and our personal information—how is it protected from hackers and such?"

"That's a very important question, Nicole," Larry said. He then detailed the firm's privacy standards, which included firewalls around all data, and testing throughout the day for any signs of a breach. He explained that this meant the highest levels of security would be implemented with all information obtained.

"I think that sums it up best," Larry said as he turned toward the CFP Board Code of Ethics hanging on the wall, and began to read Principle 5, Confidentiality: "A CFP® professional has a duty to 'protect the confidentiality of all client information.'" Larry continued to read from the document: "'A relationship of trust and confidence with the client can only be built upon the understanding that the client's information will remain confidential.' In our firm, this means that only members of our team will see your information. No one else."

"OK, I'm satisfied," said Nicole. "Where do we go from here?"

"Let me ask Paul and Joanne to come in so you can meet the rest of the team," Larry replied, and he dialed Joanne and asked her to find Paul and come with him to the conference room to meet Jessica and Nicole.

While they waited, Larry explained that he thought of planning as a "team sport." When Paul and Joanne arrived, Larry was in the middle of a short explanation of the way the planning team worked together, with each member filling a different, but complementary, role.

Nicole seemed suddenly overwhelmed by the support that was being shown for her. She pulled herself up from the chair with some effort and hugged Larry.

Jessica stood up too. "Thank you all for your help," she said.

Larry thought about mentioning that Nicole and Jessica would one day discover a soul within their plan, but as they were leaving, he was distracted by a beautiful sunset lighting up the west end of Landis Avenue. It turned the sky tangerine orange, swirling throughout pink and blue clouds, showering the flowers, plants, and all living things with a muted, whispery light. While he stood at the door of his office, waving goodbye, he could feel the pulse of their plan beating.

The radiant glow overhead signaled the end of one day and the start of the next, like the luminescence of a new plan's life.

CHAPTER 26

Larry Buys a Painting

Larry stopped by the Bell residence on his way home from the office to drop off copies of Helen's documents that he had copied and filed. Linda answered the door, and Greg came to the door as well and asked Larry if he wanted to take a quick look at his paintings.

Larry said, "Sure," and Greg led him to the shed at the rear of the house where he'd moved most of his canvases. The shed was dark, and as Larry stepped inside, he tripped and fell forward, knocking a painting to the floor.

Greg helped Larry up.

"Are you OK?" Greg said. Larry brushed off his pants, muttering apologies for being so clumsy. When he finally looked around the shed, he could see there were canvases everywhere. "Greg, this is quite a collection," Larry exclaimed. There were pictures of people, pastures, wooded scenes, and horses. To his left was a series devoted to model airplanes. "You know what I like most about your artwork, Greg?"

"What's that?" Greg asked.

"The fact that your paintings, and maybe all art as well, work in the past, present, and future at the same time. I mean, a painting is something you create in the present, and then if it's good, it inspires into the future. When it's enjoyed, it's a reflection of a past moment."

"I never thought of it like that," Greg said.

"It's actually not all that different from financial planning. We take facts from the past, talk about them in the present, and think about what they mean for the future. Do you ever think about how people in the future will experience your artwork?"

"Actually, Larry, you're right. In one of my classes, the teacher said that there is truth in beauty and beauty in truth. That's what I think about sometimes when I paint. I try to create something beautiful that is also truthful."

"There you go, it's the same in financial planning. A plan must be truthful or it will not work."

Greg looked at his work proudly, affirming the validity of Larry's statement.

"And what about the future?" Larry said. "I suppose as an artist, there's great joy in creating a work that will be appreciated forever?"

"Absolutely."

"Well, my friend, I must say that you and I are really kindred spirits," said Larry.

"How so?"

"Because as a financial planner, the work we create today of helping clients manage wealth and assets will survive for generations to come. It goes on and on, as one generation leaves their creations and accumulation to the next. It's just like the way a work of art gets passed on."

Suddenly, one of Greg's paintings caught his eye. It was simply a picture of a forest landscape, painted in rich vibrant hues of orange, green, yellow, and red. It appeared to be the edge of the forest next to a field.

"I'd like this one for the office. It would look great in the conference room."

"That's an interesting choice," Greg said, and removed the painting from the wall.

"What do you call this one?" asked Larry.

"*Landscape Number Fourteen,*" Greg said.

He carried the painting to Larry's car and Larry gave him a check.

Greg told him he wanted to save fifty percent of the sale. After depositing the check, he'd write Larry a separate check to invest.

"Good thinking," Larry said.

Larry took the painting to drop off at his office before heading home. Putting it on the wall of the conference room will create a client connection, and in financial planning, making close personal connections with clients was the fuel that propelled every successful plan.

PART FOUR

While Monitoring the Plans

CHAPTER 27

Larry Gets a Call

When Larry arrived at his office the next day, Joanne told him that Linda needed to speak to him as soon as possible. Linda's mother had to go back to the hospital because she was having trouble breathing. Linda had left a number and asked if Larry could please call.

Larry checked his schedule for the day and decided to head over to see her right away. He asked Joanne to call Linda first to let her know he was coming, and then let Paul and Barbara know that he would have to move the morning investment committee meeting to the afternoon. She said she would handle everything. Larry then grabbed Helen's file and left.

Both investments and personal circumstances are in constant motion, Larry thought as he drove to the hospital; the financial planning team must show up to work in a state of readiness to act. Proactive action is the key to fulfillment of Principle 7, Diligence, from the CFP Board Code of Ethics. It means providing "services in a reasonably prompt and thorough manner."

At the hospital, Larry received a visitor's pass and walked up to Helen's room. On the way, he saw a small flower shop in the lobby and decided to buy a bouquet of flowers.

Linda and Tom were inside the room. Helen was lying in bed, her breathing irregular and laborious. Linda smiled at Larry, but quietly pushed him and Tom out the door into the hallway, so her mother didn't wake up or overhear their discussion.

"For you," said Larry as he handed the flowers to her.

"Larry, thank you," Linda said as she took the flowers, then took a deep breath and said, "So, here we meet again."

"Yes. Tell me what's going on," Larry said with concern.

They discussed Helen's situation. The outlook was not favorable. The three doctors that had stopped by on their rounds agreed that the family should be prepared for the worst.

"Mom suffered," Linda began, and started to cry. "She had a second stroke."

Tom put his arm around her and handed her some tissues. Larry suggested that they move over to the small visitor's lobby near the elevators so they could talk.

Once seated, they began to talk about estate planning. Larry said that Helen's estate plan was in place, and that there were no end-of-life decisions that he could see; however, he suggested a call be made to an estate-planning attorney just to be certain.

Linda and Tom thought this was a good idea.

"You know, Larry, all of this has me thinking about our situation. I realize now that we really need to work on our estate planning," Linda said.

Larry had this same thing on his mind. "A financial plan, which builds wealth, must prepare for the future generations who will inherit whatever's left over," he said. "The unused wealth, so to speak."

They talked a bit about Greg and Jessica as the future generations, and then eventually the grandchildren. "Linda, don't worry," Larry said, "we'll get to it all. Right now, the focus is on your mother. Let's hope she gets out of here soon."

Larry gave Linda and then Tom a warm hug. There would eventually be much for them to do, Larry thought, but not right now. And then he said goodbye and left. He knew that when a loved one's health and welfare, perhaps her life, was at stake, any long-term planning decisions should be temporarily suspended.

CHAPTER 28

The Next Day

The next morning, Larry had breakfast with his wife and children, and got in his car to drive to his office. He backed out of the garage and was about to press the button that lowered the garage door when his cell phone rang. It was Joanne.

"Well, that's good timing, I just sat down in my car," Larry chuckled, and said good morning to Joanne.

"Good morning, Larry," she replied.

"Before I forget," he said, "can you please make a note that I have to call Mack Fletcher later today? I need him to help process a planning question about Helen's estate."

"Got it," she said, "but you may have a problem with that."

"Why's that?"

"Linda called this morning to tell you that her mother was placed on a ventilator last night. She sounded pretty upset," Joanne said.

Larry thanked Joanne for the message and immediately called Linda's cell phone. When Linda answered, he sensed she was distraught and exhausted. She told him that the hospital had called her at 3:00 a.m. to tell her that her mother was struggling to breathe. And then she began to cry.

"I'm so sorry, Linda," Larry said, and then waited for Linda to regain her composure.

"Larry, I'm sorry to cry. It's just that—with the ventilator, you know my mother never wanted to be on a machine. I spoke to the doctor and he said it might be a temporary thing. But they just don't know."

"Linda, have you called your sister with this news yet?"

"Yes," she said. "She's flying in tomorrow from Oregon and will be staying with Tom and me."

"That's good. I think it's a good thing that the family is together right now."

Linda was quiet on the other end of the receiver.

"By the way, I will be speaking to Mack later today," Larry said, "and then an estate-planning attorney to ask about any decisions that should be made at this time regarding your mother's estate. Put this out of your mind. If there's anything that needs to be done, I will call you immediately."

"Thank you, Larry," she said. "You know, there is an irony to all of this."

"What's that?"

"With all of the running around I've been doing because of Mom lately, I haven't had time to think of our finances. But I looked at our checking account yesterday, and there's over $18,000 in it. It took all of this to happen for us to have a little extra in our checking account for the first time in a while." She began to weep again.

Larry said, "Maybe other forces are guiding you."

He waited as Linda regained her composure, and then he said, "While you're with your mother at the hospital, you should tell her the good news about your saving money. I bet she would be happy to hear it."

"Do you think she'll be able to hear me?" Linda said tearfully.

"Absolutely."

"That's exactly what I'm going to do," she said. "Thanks, Larry."

Larry smiled as he hung up the phone.

CHAPTER 29

At the Office

The first thing Joanne said to Larry when he arrived at the office was that Mrs. Drusselovsky's estate planning folder was on his desk.

Larry thanked her, and asked her to hold his calls for about an hour.

"Is everything OK?" Joanne asked.

"All is fine, but I need a few minutes to write some things down."

Joanne told him she would be back in an hour. As she left, she closed his office door.

It was there, in the quiet of the morning, that Larry wrote the first chapter of his story about financial planning. Over the next several months, he would write many more chapters. After about an hour, Joanne tapped on the door.

"I wanted to let you know it's been an hour, and Mack's on the phone to talk about Helen's estate."

Larry put down his pen and picked up the phone. "Hey, Mack, what's going on?" he said.

"Larry, I looked at her will. I think we should call her lawyer, Bob Burke. He'll tell us what to do."

The issue at hand was whether there were any pre-mortem decisions that needed to be made. Though it is rare, sometimes there are issues that needed to be resolved at what may be the final moments of one's life. They conferenced Bob into the call and the three of them went over the high-level facts. Bob said that based upon the information, it did not sound as though there were any decisions that needed to be made in haste, but he qualified his answer by saying he would not render a legal opinion without seeing the entire file, and it didn't seem there was adequate time for that.

His words were enough to assure Larry and Mack. Together, they called Linda. She said she was grateful for their update, and she removed this concern from her mind.

Prompt attention to small details is the halo of all care-based financial planning.

CHAPTER 30

In the Evening

When he arrived home from work, Larry was greeted by his wife, Melissa, and their three daughters. As was their daily ritual, they sat together as a family to share the dinner meal and discuss the day's events.

After the girls took turns discussing their day at school, seven-year-old Amanda, Larry's youngest, asked her father about his day.

"Let's see," Larry said. "I helped a family put together a college plan, like we have for you guys, and I spoke to some nice people about their retirement accounts. And then, I spoke to one of my clients whose mother is in the hospital."

"What's wrong with her mother?" Amanda asked.

"Her mother is having trouble breathing, and they hooked her up to a machine so she could breathe easier. They hope she feels better."

Amanda, who was a very sensitive child, looked sad. "Why are they calling you about this? You're not a doctor."

"Well, honey, that's a good question," Larry said. "They're calling me because I'm their financial planner."

"What do you mean?" she asked.

Larry sat back in his chair and wiped his mouth with his napkin. As he took a sip of water, he thought about ways to explain to a seven-year-old what a financial planner was. "I think the best way to understand what I do is to ask you a question."

"OK," Amanda said, and smiled. "What?"

"When you see me leave in the morning to go to work, do you know where I go?"

"Yes, you go to your office," Amanda said.

"OK, that's good. Now do you know what I do when I get to the office?"

Amanda thought about it for a second, and said, "You work on stuff. Like files . . ." She thought a little more, and said, "You go on your computer. Wait, wait, you sell people insurance? Or you do stuff with money?"

It had never occurred to Larry that his kids really didn't understand what a financial planner did.

"One last question," he said. "What do Mom and I tell you to do with some of your allowance each week?"

"Take it to the bank and put it there."

"Right, but put it into what?"

"My savings account," Amanda said with pride in her voice.

"You got it, that's what I do. I help people figure out ways to save more money."

"Oh!" Amanda said in a tone that made it clear that the lightbulb of understanding had clicked on.

"And the people I help are called clients," said Larry. "A financial planner helps clients who pay him money for helping them save more money."

Amanda frowned and folded her arms.

"What's wrong, honey?" asked Larry.

"Does this mean I need to give you and Mommy some of my money because you're helping me save it?"

Larry and his wife laughed.

"Honey, no," Larry said. "Of course not. We help you free of charge."

"Yay!" Amanda cheered.

"When you're a little bit older, you can use the money in that account in any way you want. It belongs to only you."

"I love you, Daddy," she said, and then she kissed her father on the cheek and scurried away.

Larry noticed Melissa was looking at him with a loving grin. "What?" he said.

Melissa smiled and said, "You're a good daddy."

CHAPTER 31

A Week Later

With so many cases in motion at once, the week sped by quickly. Larry targeted Friday for getting caught up on everything. He spent the morning meeting with Paul and Barbara going over cases, and midday with Joanne, who helped him return calls and work on the emails filling his in-box.

When they were nearly done, Joanne said, "Larry, do you mind if I ask you a question?" She then got up from her chair and closed the door.

"Sure . . . is everything OK?" Larry asked with concern.

"We spend so much time on everyone else's financial planning, but I need some advice regarding my own." She proceeded to tell him about the situation with her own family. Her husband was disabled, and she was worried about the expenses piling up on her credit card.

So Larry spent most of the following hour with Joanne hammering out a plan to consolidate debts and develop a budget, but to not worry about savings just yet, as this was the time to try to live without incurring debt. He asked Joanne to bring all of this information into the office so he could help her put together a more thorough, detailed plan.

"I'll ask my husband to start putting it together," Joanne said.

"And then maybe he can come in and we can go over this together," Larry said.

"Thank you," Joanne said, with a look of relief on her face.

The phone rang, and as Joanne headed back to her desk to answer it, Larry reflected on the important fact that absolutely everyone needs a financial plan. It was, he realized, an essential point for his book, and as he finished writing that in his notes, Joanne returned, looking somber and concerned.

"It's Linda," Joanne said, "and it doesn't sound like good news."

Larry picked up the phone. As soon as he said hello, Linda told him that Helen had died. Over the last few days, she and her sister had agonized over whether or not to turn off the ventilator, but in the end they followed their mother's wishes. Helen had lasted for a day and then her body just gave out. "She was ready to go," Linda said with both despondency and relief in her voice.

Larry expressed his sympathy, inquired about the funeral, and then made a note to himself to make sure Joanne cleared his calendar for that day. Paul came into his office after he'd hung up the phone.

Larry shared the sad news, and said, "Financial planning is like that, isn't it Paul? It's always in motion; the present and the future, life and death."

"From what you said about Mrs. Drusselovsky's planning," Paul said, "it sounded like she was prepared for this. But even so, it's sad when someone dies."

"For the little time I knew her," Larry said, "she seemed like a lovely woman. In the end, the family followed her wishes. That's all they could do. Her goal was achieved."

"It's not easy to do what they did," Paul said.

They finished their day in the office by preparing for upcoming meetings and reviewing existing accounts.

CHAPTER 32

The Funeral

The funeral was held at graveside on a bright and sunny afternoon. Mrs. Drusselovsky had paid for the cemetery plot and the funeral arrangements in advance. The mourners and their friends gathered in the shade under a green tent next to the open grave.

Tom closed his office for a few hours and some of his staff came to pay their respects. Also, Nicole, Jessica, and the kids, along with Jess's business partner, Clarke, were there, as well as Peggy, Mack, and even Betty Ann. Next to Betty Ann stood Larry Morgan and next to him were Paul and Joanne. Barbara stayed behind to manage the office and keep an eye on things.

The funeral service was very touching and several eulogies were read. Greg and Jessica spoke eloquently about the inspiration their grandmother had been; how she was a role model for living independently and with courage. When each pledged to follow in her footsteps, Linda began to cry.

And then Linda spoke. She began by thanking everyone for coming.

"Tom and I are most appreciative to have you all here with us during this most difficult time," she said, and paused and looked at her notes. "The one thing that my mother taught me beyond all else was to be appreciative of what you have. To always be grateful and thankful for those in our lives. That people are what keep you warm, with their love and generosity. And that life was really about only two things, love and laughter."

After she shared a few stories, the clergy took over, and said some prayers as Helen's casket was lowered into the ground.

The attendees dispersed and walked slowly back to their cars. After Larry said goodbye to the familiar faces there, he gave Linda a hug. "I knew your mother only briefly, but I could tell she was very special," he said.

"Larry, thank you. I appreciate all you have done for me and my entire family over these last weeks," Linda said. Her eyes filled with tears.

"Think nothing of it," Larry said. "This is what financial planners do."

Linda smiled and said, "You know something, Larry? I think I finally realize what you have been saying all along about the soul of my financial plan."

"What's that?"

"I finally get it."

"How so?"

"It's this," she said, pointing to herself and then to Larry, back and forth. "This is the soul of my plan. It's you. Being here today and being present for me and my family over these last weeks. Helping us get things together and organized. Running all of those reports. But really, more than anything I realize now that the soul of a financial plan exists when you realize how much your planner really cares about you. That's it, that's the soul of a financial plan."

"Thank you," said Larry with a humble smile.

Linda hugged him again and turned to say goodbye to the others.

Larry drove home with memories of Mrs. Drusselovsky and a life well lived firmly planted in his heart and mind.

CHAPTER 33

A Few Weeks Later

"Well, do I have everything I need?" Larry asked Joanne.

"Yes, it's all there in the file—your fact finder, your risk tolerance questionnaire, and your sample financial plan," she said as she handed him the file.

"Perfect, thank you," said Larry.

He walked quickly down the hallway and asked Paul if he was ready to meet the Smith family. The Smiths owned a third-generation family business that sold an industrial lubricant used in making machine parts. Larry and Paul had been referred to them by Clarke Addison, who had been pleased with the business planning process he and Jessica had completed for their dental office.

"Larry, I'm ready," Paul said. "Let's meet the Smiths."

"On to the next one," Larry said, while speed walking down the hall with his wheeled brief case in tow. It was time to begin a new financial plan—the start of a new life, a new soul, and a new adventure.

Epilogue

There is a moment in every kitchen table financial plan when the soul of the plan is born. It happens when a client realizes how much his or her planner cares about their choices, their future, and their well-being. The planner's commitment to the client's success forms the nucleus of every successful financial plan.

But deeper within the biology of a plan, there is another critical element, a life force, the mitochondria that gives the plan its energy and moves it toward the clients' goals and dreams. It's a spirit, simple and pure.

And that spirit is hope.

Hope is an action word—we hope for the economy to flourish and for our investments to go up in value. Or we hope to remain in good health so we can continue working. But hope is also a state of being. It is optimism, promise, and confidence, all combined together.

The process of financial planning is not about finding hope. Usually, hope is present from the beginning. Rather, planning uses the energy of hope to move closer to a future goal or dream. If there is a possibility that a goal can be achieved, then the planner's analysis will reveal it, and the client will feel hopeful.

However, if the analysis reveals that a goal is out of reach, the planner must be forthright with the truth. The success or failure of a relationship between client and planner does not rest upon market-based performance; it rests upon integrity in the pursuit of goals and objectives.

For many, just knowing they are not alone in the vast, intimidating world of financial markets and perplexing tax laws is comforting. To have a guide with you is of great value when the markets are correcting downward. When pessimism comes and when all hope is lost, the financial planner helps to manage the emotions that accompany lost hope.

The question will come again: Where am I going?

To restore faith and confidence, the very best remedy is a review meeting in which the planner and the client get together. In a meeting, facts and emotions can be vetted, success or failure in future goals can be gauged, and hope can be restored.

Acting alone is not what kitchen table financial planning is about. It's about traveling together as companions on a journey, a journey not taken out of a sense of duty or personal reward, but because of friendship and a love of travel.

Traveling with a friend is a wonderful joy!

Code of Ethics and Professional Responsibility

CFP Board adopted the Code of Ethics to establish the highest principles and standards. These principles are general statements expressing the ethical and professional ideals certificants and registrants are expected to display in their professional activities. As such, the principles are aspirational in character and provide a source of guidance for certificants and registrants. The principles form the basis of CFP Board's *Rules of Conduct, Practice Standards* and *Disciplinary Rules*, and these documents together reflect CFP Board's recognition of certificants' and registrants' responsibilities to the public, clients, colleagues and employers.

PRINCIPLE 1—INTEGRITY:
Provide professional services with integrity.

Integrity demands honesty and candor, which must not be subordinated to personal gain and advantage. Certificants are

The code is available at the CFP® website: https://www.cfp.net/for-cfp -professionals/professional-standards-enforcement/standards-of-professional -conduct/code-of-ethics-professional-responsibility.

placed in positions of trust by clients, and the ultimate source of that trust is the certificant's personal integrity. Allowance can be made for innocent error and legitimate differences of opinion, but integrity cannot co-exist with deceit or subordination of one's principles.

PRINCIPLE 2—OBJECTIVITY:
Provide professional services objectively.

Objectivity requires intellectual honesty and impartiality. Regardless of the particular service rendered or the capacity in which a certificant functions, certificants should protect the integrity of their work, maintain objectivity and avoid subordination of their judgment.

PRINCIPLE 3—COMPETENCE:
Maintain the knowledge and skill necessary to provide professional services competently.

Competence means attaining and maintaining an adequate level of knowledge and skill, and application of that knowledge and skill in providing services to clients. Competence also includes the wisdom to recognize the limitations of that knowledge and when consultation with other professionals is appropriate or referral to other professionals necessary. Certificants make a continuing commitment to learning and professional improvement.

PRINCIPLE 4—FAIRNESS:

Be fair and reasonable in all professional relationships. Disclose conflicts of interest.

Fairness requires impartiality, intellectual honesty and disclosure of material conflicts of interest. It involves a subordination of one's own feelings, prejudices and desires so as to achieve a proper balance of conflicting interests. Fairness is treating others in the same fashion that you would want to be treated.

PRINCIPLE 5—CONFIDENTIALITY:

Protect the confidentiality of all client information.

Confidentiality means ensuring that information is accessible only to those authorized to have access. A relationship of trust and confidence with the client can only be built upon the understanding that the client's information will remain confidential.

PRINCIPLE 6—PROFESSIONALISM:

Act in a manner that demonstrates exemplary professional conduct.

Professionalism requires behaving with dignity and courtesy to clients, fellow professionals, and others in business-related activities. Certificants cooperate with fellow certificants to enhance and maintain the profession's public image and improve the quality of services.

PRINCIPLE 7—DILIGENCE:

Provide professional services diligently.

Diligence is the provision of services in a reasonably prompt and thorough manner, including the proper planning for, and supervision of, the rendering of professional services.

Recommended Reading

Siddhartha by Herman Hesse

Abundance by Peter H. Diamandis & Steven Kotler

A New Earth by Eckhart Tolle

How to Find the Work You Love by Laurence G. Boldt

The Art of Loving by Erich Fromm

How Full Is Your Bucket? by Tom Rath and Donald O. Clifton

The Swiss Secret to Optimal Health: Dr. Rau's Diet for Whole Body Healing by Thomas Rau and Susan M. Wyler

How to Retire Happy, Wild, and Free by Ernie J. Zelinski

Love Your Neighbor by Zelig Pliskin

It's Our Ship by Captain D. Michael Abrashoff

Psycho-Cybernetics by Maxwell Maltz

Acknowledgments

My wife, Suzanne, without your encouragement and understanding, it would have been hard to keep writing, rewriting, and writing again.

All of my wonderful clients, without you this story could not exist.

The team at Levy & Associates, thank you for your countless hours of support and togetherness. We are a financial planning family.

Thank you to Mike, Don, Joe, Donna, Judith, and Jackie for being my friends and my character inspirations.

My family—Mom, Dad, Sue, and David—thank you all for your trust and support.

Buz, thank you for your continued mentorship.

My first draft editing team—Marlene Adelstein, Susan Krawitz, Marsha Z. Dollinger, Judith Trojnar, and Jessica Carter—thank you all for taking the time to read my work and offering your kind suggestions.

My new friends at Greenleaf Book Group, LLC, thank you for your professionalism and enthusiasm. To the talented Elizabeth Brown—great job working together on the edits. To

Sally Garland and Jen Glynn, thanks for keeping this process moving along.

My boys, Ben, Jonathan, and Lewis, thank you for understanding that Dad is always thinking and moving, except when he is living in the present moment (which I hope is always).

Author Q & A

Q: Completing your first book must feel gratifying. Can you discuss some of the joys and challenges of this experience?

A: Writing a book has been unlike any other experience. First, finding the time to write was an enormous challenge. I usually wrote very early in the morning, before the workday began. The most challenging part of the process for me was maintaining the continuity of the story from one day to the next. However, the greatest joy would come from meeting with my clients during the day and then incorporating the real life interactions into the story line. Many of the incidents captured in the book are reflective of these real life experiences. I have a feeling that when they read the book, many of my clients will see bits and pieces of themselves in the various scenes.

Q: You've received a breadth of educational degrees—from English literature to accounting to law school. How and why did you settle on working as a CERTIFIED FINANCIAL PLANNER™ professional?

A: When I first discovered financial planning nearly twenty years ago, everything clicked for me. For much of my life, I did not truly know what my career path would be. I was definitely not one of those kids who knew what they were going to be when they grew up. As I got older in the profession, I found it to be a good fit for me because it incorporated all of my educational training into one discipline, and I like that I am constantly learning new things.

Q: You might say that your primary reason for working with clients is to help them achieve financial stability. What do you think are the main causes for instability in individual or family finances?

A: One of the hardest things to overcome in any financial plan is poor spending habits. Creating governance and discipline around spending is critical to success. This goes hand in hand with debt management. In general, people who struggle with spending are often carrying a large debt load as well. But I also think people struggle to keep their finances organized. I find that a failure to organize often leads to financial instability.

Q: The characters in this book, with the exception of young Greg, have more resources to work with than the average American. Can you still help folks who haven't been as good at saving as, say, the Bells or Mrs. Drusselovsky?

A: We work with all kinds of clients in our office. In fact, the very best part of our practice is our dedication to multigenerational planning. Whenever we can, we try to work with our clients' parents and their children too. I believe everybody needs financial planning on some level.

Q: What if a person feels it's too late to start saving, or their income is too low and they need all their income just to pay their bills? It can seem tough to get started.

A: The process of getting started begins with a conversation between the client and the financial planner. The first goals have to be identified. There is usually some sort of challenge, whether it's starting a late savings program or dealing with challenging income. In each situation, people have the desire for financial security in some way and it is the financial planner's job to identify the challenges and try to come up with strategies to address them.

Q: If you could give only one piece of advice to someone wishing to gain greater financial stability, what would it be?

A: Start the process of financial planning today. Beginning as early as possible is the key to a successful long-term financial plan. Financial planners need the longevity of time to allow resources to build and savings plans to work. I encourage all people who do not have a plan to get started now, as it only gets more difficult the later you begin.

Q: You named this book for the kitchen table, where you say the best planning can happen. What can you do in a person's kitchen that you can't do in an office conference room?

A: For me, the kitchen table is a very sacred place. There's a certain energy there where people are relaxed and able to really talk about how they feel concerning their finances. For many people, dealing with their finances is a constant source of anxiety, but sitting at the kitchen table alleviates a lot of that fear. I find that most people think of it as a safe place.

Q: In your experience, what is the most common mistake people make regarding their personal finances? And can you set us straight on how to correct that?

A: The single biggest mistake people make when it comes to their personal finances is not connecting their resources together with their goals. Most people are either spending without any awareness of savings, or they're saving without any awareness of their goals. I say start with the goal and then work backward. That is the surest way to avoid making mistakes.

Q: What is something that has surprised you in your work as a CFP® professional?

A: I find it surprising that more people don't engage in financial planning. So many people are satisfied simply to have an investment advisor, even if that advisor doesn't connect investment management to financial planning goals and objectives. I am also surprised that so many investment advisors don't connect wealth management with a comprehensive financial plan. Connecting both elements together is the alchemy of financial security.

Q: What do you love most about your work as a CFP® professional? What do you least enjoy?

A: This is an easy question. I absolutely enjoy meeting with people, reviewing their plans, and talking to them about their futures. It is such a satisfying feeling to help people in this way, and I know how much my clients have come to rely on my team and me. For me, the least enjoyable part of the job (which my team really helps me with) is all the data crunching and file management. We deal heavily with information, and without my team of associates assisting in this manner, I could not do my job nearly as well.

Q: Some people may think they can handle their own finances—planning, budgeting, setting up savings, etc. Do you agree, or do you believe everyone would benefit from visiting a CFP® professional? What might those do-it-yourselfers be missing out on? Can you actually save them more money than they can save without your help?

A: I think there are certain parts of finance that people can deal with on their own. For example, I think it is possible for individuals to do a fairly good job of buying something like car insurance on their own. However, putting together all the varied pieces of tax law, insurance, and investments requires specialized training. Especially when it comes to planning around death issues; this is clearly an area where people need help. I think over the long run, the small fee that people pay for financial planning pales in comparison to the amount of value they receive around financial security and the protection of assets.

Q: In the book, Larry decides to buy Linda and Tom a small piggy bank—as an impetus to get them to start saving. Can you elaborate on this?

A: I like this scene. When I meet people like the Bells who are really challenged with developing a savings strategy, I think I serve the function of a coach, like in sports. The gift of the piggy bank is really just a nice way to say that I am committed to your savings strategy and with your acceptance of this gift, you are committing, too. In my practice, I have not ever given a client a piggy bank, but I really like the way this plays out in the story. I might actually start doing it.

Q: These days many of us have instant access to 24/7 online shopping (spending) with our phones. This can be so tempting! Have you seen a decrease in savings since smartphones have become so widespread?

A: I don't think I've seen any palpable change in spending due to the online revolution and smartphones, but I do think they lull us into a certain way of thinking. We become so accustomed to instant gratification of information that when it comes to wanting to buy something, we are more at risk for impulse shopping. I know with many of my clients and including myself, we sometimes find ourselves shopping for items late at night or early in the morning. I think this is the beginning of a trend that could impact people's savings habits down the road. I especially worry about young people, who spend so much time in activities that rely on instant gratification.

Q: Have you ever worked with clients saddled with heavy debt? If they think their situation is hopeless, how do you get them to take that first step on the road to financial equilibrium?

A: Working with clients who have heavy debts is a very difficult proposition. Usually this is a sign that they don't govern their spending habits. But there are many older clients who come to our firm with substantial debt, but who also have sizeable retirement assets. This combination is typical because even clients with spending issues know they cannot spend their retirement plan assets—or else taxes and penalties may apply. The ones I really worry about, though, are the younger clients who put themselves through college and graduate school. It takes a firm commitment to reduce that debt burden and eventually turn the tide toward building a savings plan. A simple formula: Time + Dedication = Savings.

Q: Finally, if you could name the single most important idea you want readers to remember from your book, what would it be and why?

A: Patience is the foundation of a good financial plan. As noted in the book, Larry and his team never move quickly through problems or situations. Everything is planned; even little things or simple questions are always prepared in advance. I think that when you work with a financial planner, you have to recognize that things happen in slow, methodical steps. That is the very best way to avoid making mistakes and to establish the best approaches to handling problems and working toward goals.

Q: Most people are very private about their finances. How do you encourage someone who might be too afraid to come to you—out of fear, worry, shame, etc.?

A: I think this is a good question. I find that when you begin with something intangible as a first step, it helps get over the fear and shame. For example, planning for the possibility of unexpected death is a way to overcome these emotions. If we address death planning first, which involves protecting spouses and children, it gets people comfortable with planning. The same holds true with other types of risk like the risk of losing work income because of a disability, or the risk of needing an expensive operation. Both risks involve insurance planning, disability insurance, and health insurance. This eases people in, and continues to remain an important component of financial planning. Of the many clients I help today, many began this way, focused upon one aspect of insurance planning, and then we build from there.

About the Author

Victor Levy is a CERTIFIED FINANCIAL PLANNER™ practitioner and president of Levy & Associates, a wealth management and employee benefits company located in Philadelphia. Victor received a BA in English literature from Boston University; a JD from the John Marshall Law School in Chicago, Illinois; a LLM from the University of Miami School of Law in Coral Gables, Florida; and he holds the CLU designation from The American College of Financial Services in Bryn Mawr, Pennsylvania. He fills his days working with families to help them develop, maintain, and prepare for life's journeys and contingencies, and he does it all with one goal in mind—to bring about their financial security.

On a personal note, Victor and his wife, Suzanne, reside in Cherry Hill, New Jersey. They have three children, Benjamin, Jonathan, and Lewis, and they are both active members in their community. In his spare time, Victor enjoys spending time with his wife and sons, reading, and exercising.

CPSIA information can be obtained at www.ICGtesting.com
Printed in the USA
BVOW08*0959190916

461973BV00003B/1/P